running your ROCK BAND

running your
ROCK BAND

- rehearsing
- financing
- touring
- succeeding

bill henderson

SCHIRMER BOOKS

New York

Schirmer Books

1633 Broadway
New York, New York 10019

Library of Congress Catalog Card Number: 96-7282

Printed in the United States of America

Printing Number
  3 4 5 6 7 8 9 10

Library of Congress Cataloging-in-Publication Data

Henderson, William.
    Running your rock band : rehearsing, financing, touring,
  succeeding / Bill Henderson.
        p. cm.
    Includes bibliographical references and index.
    ISBN 0-02-864611-8 (alk. paper)
    1. Rock music—Vocational guidance. 2. Rock music—Economic
  aspects. I. Title.
  ML3795.H447 1996
  781.66'023—dc20   96-7282
                                                            CIP
                                                            MN

This paper meets the requirements of ANSI/NISO Z39.48.1992 (Pemanence of Paper).

contents

	INTRODUCTION	vii
1	GETTING STARTED	1
2	WOODSHEDDING: THIRTY DAYS TO A WORKING BAND	11
3	HOW TO RUN YOUR OWN BOOKING OPERATION	21
4	IMAGES AND AGENTS	31
5	DEVELOPING A FOLLOWING	43
6	CLUBS, COLLEGES, CONCERTS	51
7	BASIC SHOWMANSHIP	61
8	BASIC MUSICIANSHIP	69
9	BOOZE AND DOPE	79
10	THE STUDIO	85
11	EQUIPMENT	97
12	THE ROADIE	107
13	MONEY AND THE BAND	117
14	ON THE ROAD	125
15	CHANGING AND REBUILDING	135
16	MANAGERS AND MANAGEMENT	141
17	THE RECORD DEAL	157
	AFTERWORD	165
	GLOSSARY	169
	SELECT BIBLIOGRAPHY	173
	INDEX	177

introduction

I f a new band falters and fails, it is often because of the ambiguous nature of the undertaking. A band is both an artistic venture and a business. If both ends are well attended to, the result is success. If either esthetics or commerce is neglected, the band will go under; it's as simple as that. Regrettably, it's a rare personality that combines both musicianship and business skill in equal proportions. Music, of course, is what you want to spend your time on, yet we've all heard bands that made good music—and a month or so later they were defunct. On the other hand, many bands have built long and lucrative careers with a combination of modest talent and sharp business heads. Knowing how to do it is the crucial difference.

A band can be all things to all people: it is a business; the center of a small society; a technological undertaking; a way of showing off; a collaborative artistic venture; a trade or skill; and, at its best, a powerful symbol of forces vulgar and beautiful that give the present day much of its character. A band is an eminently worthwhile undertaking, and so this book says: don't wait—do it! But do it right to maximize the pleasure, and minimize the pain. This book will help take you where you want to go.

1

GETTING STARTED

WHO'S IN CHARGE?
A BAND MUST HAVE A LEADER

Lack of leadership is a legacy of the long-gone "do your own thing" days of the '60s, when you weren't supposed to want to be a leader. I've seen bands paralyzed because no one would step out and assume leadership, nor would they let anybody else try it. That philosophy just doesn't work. Any group enterprise as complex as a working band must have somebody behind the wheel or it won't go; there must be a leader.

If that leader is you, you are either boss or first-among-equals. You've either put the band together in the first place or have emerged as its dominant personality. You are entrusted to make decisions for the band and take responsibility for their outcome. Your imagination and energy, more than anyone else's, will guide the band's destiny. This book is primarily addressed to you, the leader.

Now, the fact is, a band is a bunch of ornery individualists who generally won't be dictated to. This is not the era of the company man, not in rock 'n' roll; so a leader must use authority carefully. It's best if he (or she) is both the musical and the business head, but often this is not the case, nor is it always necessary. The two functions can be split, as long as everyone understands and abides by the rules. If, as leader, you are uncomfortable handling important business matters, you should try letting another band member oversee money and bookings. This can work well—except that when people approach you to discuss business, your ego may not allow you to refer them to the business manager. The result can be lost bookings and confusion, until you realize it just isn't in your best interest to short-circuit the system. People will always approach the visible leader with propositions. If this is you, your ego must be strong enough to turn them over to the band member who handles the business. Ideally, your position should be that of a top executive, watching over everything, but not necessarily doing it all.

But in large matters the final decisions have to be yours. On stage and off, your influence must add up to the difference between form and anarchy. You become a target for praise and blame, and consequently, you must prepare yourself to be alternately loved and hated by the band.

CHOOSE YOUR PARTNERS CAREFULLY

Bands can come together in any number of ways. Sometimes the remains of an old band—the bass player, drummer, and a keyboard player, let's say—form a new one. A manager or agent may "package" a band and send if off on the road immediately. Often a lead vocalist assembles a backup band; sometimes he or she is a writer-performer with no band experience.

Be sure of one thing: no matter how it starts, a band is a long-term partnership. You can count on one to three years of hard labor before it begins to pay off. When it does, the living is good, but you should consider carefully who you want to spend your scuffling days with. Choose with care, preferably among those you know and have worked with before. The fewer unknown factors you face, the more stable the band is likely to be.

Before you consider working with total strangers, exhaust your personal contacts. Look around: Who's free now? Who's just come off the road looking for a local gig? Who's unhappy with a present band? If you are considering musicians you don't know personally, find out all you can about them. Do they have erratic natures? Bad habits? How much band experience has each of them had? Knowing about their personalities in advance is valuable; it could save you pain, money, lost time, and lost energy farther down the line.

Be aware, though, that working with close friends can be just as explosive as working with total strangers. Under stress, even good friends can become hostile or uncooperative, so maintaining basic congeniality is important. If somebody is irritating you for no reason, look out—it will only get worse.

Your ambitions, desires, and goals should match up. Some band members may want to gravitate to a big city—New York,

Boston, Chicago—braving high-cost living and little or no pay to be closer to the heart of the big-league music business. Some may want to be where a "scene" is established or developing: Seattle, Austin, Chapel Hill. (Here the priority is not so much earning a full-time living, but to make your mark, with original material, on that particular scene.) Some may simply want to earn a steady living, to exploit all available avenues for paying gigs in the local area, be it Cedar Rapids, Bangor, Biloxi, or Peoria. (If this book has a bias, it's toward the latter situation, by far the most common one across the country, although nearly everything here applies equally to any new band struggling to establish itself.)

In any case, all potential conflicts should be raised and aired: if you intend for the band to work locally, but your prospective drummer wants to hit the road for Colorado, it's not going to last long. Find out about these matters and discuss them carefully up front.

Watch out for age differences. If you're a twenty-one-year-old singer, your view of the future will probably be different from a thirty-two-year-old guitar player's (not necessarily, but look out for it). You must have some agreement, at the start, on the style and direction the band will follow. Without it you'll never achieve a musical identity. It's not an absolute necessity to like the same music: sometimes interesting composite sounds emerge from bands of musicians with different tastes. But there should be some basic respect for the *quality* of one another's taste. If you secretly think your guitar player can't discriminate between good music and trash, it will be difficult for you to work together. Better to avoid that by linking up with someone whose taste matches your own.

The same goes for instrumental or vocal skill. If you believe candidates for your band are weak musically and won't improve, turn them down. Otherwise you'll always hold it against them for not being able to play what you want to hear. Result: hostility, and over a long period of time, decay of the band's ability to grow and communicate on even the most basic matters, musical or otherwise.

Communication is the most difficult and constant hassle you will face. And you will have to face it—among yourselves, between you and your audience, and you and your business contacts. Musically it can amount to a virtual Pandora's box, because in rock 'n' roll there is no orthodoxy—no single language, no level of knowledge that all must attain before they start working. In the same band you might have conservatory graduates working with musicians who don't know the first thing about music theory. How do we talk about nuts and bolts?

Classical music has a precise and exact language for everything. Not only that, there are well-established hierarchies of communication that make working together in classical ensembles pretty efficient. Classical ensembles, however, are always working off the page; the piece is finished, and the only problem is to read the score correctly and put all the parts together.

Rock 'n' roll musicians work under a double handicap. First, they don't have a standard musical language and therefore find it hard to talk to one another about what they want to do. Second, what they do requires just such a language because they must work improvisationally, creating the piece as they work. They *must* talk to one another! Find a common language as soon as you can; sit down and work it out. You'll thank yourself a thousand times once you begin rehearsals.

SOME TROUBLE AREAS

The items that follow may seem trivial, especially in the first romantic blush of a new band, but look out: they can turn into monsters!

Communication

It's a good idea to institute a weekly band meeting right away. Later, as band affairs become murkier, and various band members begin to turn up with their gripes, the meeting is a good format to clear the air. Rehearsals or gigs don't seem conducive to this kind of discussion, so it's best not to try and combine the meeting with some other function.

Sometimes band meetings don't get off the ground, due to a tendency to avoid confronting difficult matters. Don't lay back in these meetings. Get an informal agenda together and go through it, item by item. Make sure nobody's gripe escapes discussion. Repressed or unexpressed gripes become smoldering grudges, wedges that can split the band apart. Everything must be aired. The weekly band meeting should be an institution. Later on, weekly paychecks can be written out at this time. Have it around noon, in your favorite bar. It can actually be pleasant. But remember—it's a family meeting. Tell strangers and friends to take a walk while the meeting is in progress.

Transportation

From the moment of its inception, a new band will be coming together at least several times a week for rehearsals and gigs. Usually, those who have transportation end up providing wheels for those who don't. This is perhaps as it should be, yet the "haves" invariably end up busting their tails for the "have nots." You end up having conversations that sound like this:

"You guys knew I'd need transportation; that was one of the conditions when I joined the band."

"Okay, granted, but it's gotten ridiculous. We miscalculated, we admit it, but you'll have to handle it yourself from now on."

If you don't have transportation, try your best to get it, or to handle the problem yourself in some way. If you do ride with someone else, offer to pay your share of gas and tolls; don't wait to be asked. And return the favor when you can.

Living

Musicians move around a lot. When a band is formed, there is always a temptation to house everybody in one location: rent a big house out in the suburbs, share the bills, and rehearse in the basement. Beware. Unless people know one another through and through—and even then—this kind of arrangement can cause fatal stresses. It's hard enough for people to live together at all without adding constant work strains to the situation. Imagine being intensely angry with one of your roommates who owes you fifty dollars, doesn't have the rent this month, and left a pile of dirty dishes in the sink last night—and now you have to go downstairs and rehearse together for four hours! When there's no escape, the band can become the seventh circle of hell. What's the point anymore?

Sex

That is, gender. A sexually mixed band often risks trouble down the line because the two sexes just can't seem to keep their hands off each other. The aftermath of sexual involvement with another band member is usually wicked. So proceed with caution. In general, resist rather than encourage lust; try to find carnal happiness outside the band. Mixing genders in the band can do wonders for both your music and your business. If you can make it work, you may have something special. Just be aware of the difficulties.

MAKE YOUR MATERIAL
INTERESTING AND EFFECTIVE

No matter how good the players in your band are, it's your material that testifies to your brilliance—or lack of it. For a new band, the choice of material is crucial. It's going to take a while to find an image and performing style both comfortable and complimentary to you, a group of individuals. But without good material, it'll take even longer. The material you choose should help this process, not work against it. You can't always include your favorite numbers; some of them may simply be wrong for this band. Take a step back, as you evaluate your material, and consider what best suits your band. Be shrewd. Be practical. But in the end, your taste has to be your guide. Don't do numbers that you feel weird about.

Remember: you want to make people happy. If your attitude toward your audience is hostile or remote, you shouldn't be a performer. That doesn't mean you have to pander to them; you shouldn't be so weak as to run out and do *anything* any audience seems to want. What you actually perform will express a delicate balance—your perception of what you are, the audience's perception of what you are, and an unspoken agreement that you are in charge of the show.

In most cases you'll want to play dance music if you can, because the average bar crowd will be all over you if you don't. If a large proportion of your material can be easily danced to, you are taking the simplest route to audience excitement. They'll be up and moving, getting hot and thirsty, and you'll get lots of work. You needn't be limited by it; if you feel that a vein of nondanceable new-wave music is right for you, don't force yourselves to suppress it. In the end, audiences will come to hear you because you are you.

Some songs are definitely danceable, some are not. Analyze the good ones, the ones that bring fifty people up to the dance floor in seconds flat. What kinds of beats are danceable? Look for variety; avoid monotony. The same beat, song after song, will soon tire people and bore them as well. Four or five numbers back-to-back without a change of key is not a good idea. Watch carefully what happens when you start each of your numbers. Do people sit down? Do you hold their attention, or do they start talking and wandering around? You should constantly evaluate your material in terms of audience response.

There will always be individuals in the crowd who want to hear the chestnuts, the most threadbare, worked-to-death standards. For many years "Proud Mary" headed the list. I've never been in a band that really wanted to perform "Proud Mary," but I suppose I could play it in my sleep. Avoid building the core of your repertoire out of chestnuts. I'm not saying you should avoid familiar numbers—you can use a certain amount of familiarity to build excitement—just try not to do the same ones that every band does. And don't be apologetic about telling persistent fans, "We don't do it." They represent only a small part of your audience, anyway; you're a band, not a jukebox.

Covers

To work the lounges, parties, and frat houses, you've got to play "cover versions" of the popular hits by other bands. Even if performing originals is your ultimate goal, remember this: no working band fills its calendar on originals alone—not until the most advanced stages of its career. Everybody starts by doing other people's music. If you approach it in the right way, you can turn a repertoire of covers into your own unique body of material. There are three basic kinds of covers: imitations, rearrangements, and medleys.

IMITATIONS

You want these to sound like the original; you are literally imitating the sound of the recording. If your band is attempting to break into a predominantly "Classic Rock" or "Top 40" market, you'll want to play a lot of these. If you intend to try something more specialized, there's still nothing wrong with including a few imitations. Sometimes you start with an imitation and do it so well it becomes better than the record! But if you're aiming for the top, and hoping to break nationally, avoid slavish imitations, especially of bands in your special field—you'll be aping your competition, something no band with recording ambitions should ever do.

When choosing imitations, consider carefully your similarity, or lack of it, to the original. Don't attempt a flashy number if you'll look ridiculous in comparison with the original artist. If you can't handle a crucial instrumental solo, if you can't sing the vocal part, if you can't strut, dance, or scream like James Brown, better try to find something else. I've seen a lot of otherwise decent bands look absurd when they tore into an ill-advised imitation.

REARRANGEMENTS

Here you take a number and view it from a different angle; you alter the beat, change the mood, or make it seem to say something else. You rearrange it in your own style. Rearrangements are your chance to have your cake and eat it, too; you start with a number that's tested and proven, and you work your creative magic on it to come up with something "original." Rearrangements are good for you—often better than your own originals (unless your originals are absolutely tops).

Half the fun is in the chase: rearrangements can be really satisfying to discover. Be a collector—or at least a connoisseur. Turn your attention to your old record collection; listen again to cuts you haven't heard for years. Check out old singles. Find old records that nobody else has or remembers. Look especially for crossovers and updates. If you can find a country & western or rhythm 'n' blues cut that can cross over into a rock format, you've struck gold. Likewise, if you can find an oldie that can be recast in your style, it's a gem.

An important rule is: listen to the radio. Listen constantly. Flip the dial. Hit the oldies stations, the C&W stations, the R&B stations, the Classic Rock and Top 40 stations. These are your sources; keep up with them. Listen with a purpose: to find material for your band.

MEDLEYS

These are the greatest crowd-pleasers you can use. Build them around an artist or a band. For example, the Elvis medley, the Chuck Berry medley, the Van Halen medley, and so on. Medleys are limited only by your imagination and your audience's tolerance for the subject. You can also base a medley on a particular style, to contrast with your own style, as a novelty or change of pace. A rock band might do a "country" medley, a country-rock band might do a "blues" medley. This gives the band a chance to show off what they can do in another vein.

In general, medleys are popular with audiences, usually good for dancing, always good for pacing and set-building. You should have two or three of them.

Sample Medleys

By artist:
A Chuck Berry medley: "Roll Over Beethoven"/"Memphis Tennessee"/"Rock & Roll Music"/"Johnny B. Goode"

By style:
Blues medley: "Little Red Rooster" (Howlin' Wolf, Rolling Stones)/"The Thrill Is Gone" (B. B. King)/"Stormy Monday" (Willie Dixon, Bobby Bland)

By period:
  '50s medley: "Chantilly Lace" (Big Bopper)/"Blue Suede Shoes" (Carl Perkins, Elvis Presley)/"Sweet Little Sixteen" (Chuck Berry)/"Summertime Blues" (Eddie Cochran)

Original material

Be careful. Very little original material is good enough to justify its existence—and this is bound to include yours, too. Don't be upset if club owners tell you they're not interested in your originals "so keep playing covers." Just nod, agree, and keep on slipping your originals in there. Perform 15 to 20 percent original material a night at first.

Keep to your strongest stuff. Don't use weak or even just so-so original material. Study the crowd's reaction to it. If an original stinks, throw it out and try another one in its place. Don't be deluding yourself on how good your stuff is if nobody else likes it. That's a trap—for your personality as well as for your professional judgment. If you're blind to your shortcomings, you will never grow, improve, or get anywhere. Remember, you're not a genius yet (if you are, overlook that remark). Learn from criticism. Don't be defensive.

If you're trying to produce good originals, learn the forms. Find out how a good song is made. Listen to the radio. Analyze what you hear. Commercial successes are almost always written by time-tested pros. What do they do? Take those songs apart to see what makes them tick. How many verses? Is there a chorus? Is the chorus in a different key from the verse? What's the "hook"—the crucial element that makes the song stick in your mind? Listen to the less-commercial master songwriters: Paul Simon, Randy Newman, Elvis Costello. What do they do? Check out bad stuff, too. Why is it bad? In some ways you can learn more by analyzing bad songs than good songs (the better they are, the more invisible their seams).

In your own writing, imitate the songs you like. Don't be afraid to do this—you can learn by imitation, even though you will often encounter the following attitude: "Don't imitate other songwriters. You'll ruin your art, you'll crush your creativity." But in your early stages, you *must* imitate. That's the only way to learn this tricky art. Be aware, however, that imitation is an exercise: do it until you get the idea, then concentrate on expressing what's in your own head.

When new material is introduced to the band, take special care to arrange it thoroughly and with the utmost creative concentration. Why? Because unlike covers, originals have not been arranged previously by someone else; no recorded arrangement already exists for you to steal from, alter, or rearrange. You're on your own—you must build an arrangement from the ground up. You want your original material to sound terrific. Ironically, in many bands the originals are duller than the covers because the band forgot it had to make that extra effort. Don't let this happen. Arrange your originals with loving care.

One final word about originals: copyright them! Don't ever perform an original in public without copyrighting it first. Before you've done this, the song does not legally belong to you and can be legally stolen.

Now, if your nose is ready for the grindstone, press on. Chapter 2 deals with the most crucial weeks in a new band's genesis.

2

WOODSHEDDING: THIRTY DAYS TO A WORKING BAND

You *can* be "a working band" in thirty days, provided you have the time, the energy, and the place to put it all together. You may not be "the tightest of bands," but you will be ready to work. You will never again undergo such a concentrated working experience, so make the best of it. If it goes sour, you'll all end up hating one another. If it goes smoothly, you've got a band—fresh, strong, and ready to work.

Because total immersion is the most efficient way to learn thirty-five or forty numbers, you'll face the temptation to get away from it all and put the band under one roof. Remember this note of caution: it may work beautifully, but be prepared for the tensions that will accumulate if the living is difficult. A better situation would be the exclusive use of an industrial loft or warehouse space, on a twenty-four-hour-a-day-access schedule. You can work four hours a day, eight hours a day, or more, at loud volume levels, and go home when it's all over. Whatever you choose, the space should be secure, so you can leave equipment set up. If you must set up and tear down every time you rehearse, it will drive you crazy. I hate to sound unromantic, but the secret of preparing a large amount of material quickly and thoroughly is *efficiency*. Plan your period of preparation as if it were a space mission. Everyone in the band should know what's coming up on any given day. You can even lay out your whole rehearsal plan ahead of time.

Buy a large wall calendar—the biggest kind, with boxes 2 × 2 inches for each day of the month. Work out a schedule that introduces, say, three new numbers a day, then review them regularly. Set aside part of the rehearsal for learning new numbers, and part for reviewing the numbers you learned yesterday or the day before. Every third day should be for review, especially once you've learned over ten or fifteen numbers.

Regular review is vital. The worst possible thing you can do is learn a number, then let it sit for two weeks without rehearsing it. It's a complete drain of time and energy, because you will have to learn it all over again. When you begin playing out, you will run through your material in the course of a night's work and review won't be so necessary—but you're not working yet.

To help each player review at home, everyone should have a portable cassette recorder—a cheap one will do. Once a new number has been set, reach down and punch the "record" button during a run-through. That night, plug in your headphones and play along with the cassette.

This individual homework really speeds up the preparation period. If you have trouble remembering chord changes, for example, write them down in a notebook and drill yourself on them at home. Don't wait to relearn them at the next run-through; that just wastes everybody's time, yours included. Morale is important during this period. It's easy to bog down and fall behind schedule, and depressing when it happens. It won't happen if you don't let it.

Arrangements should be worked on in stages or levels. A good procedure is to break down each number into its basic components, as if you were preparing to go into a sixteen-track recording studio.

Sample Rehearsal Schedule

1. Listen to two Bruce Springsteen standards ("Born to Run"; "Dancing in the Dark")

   Try duplicating his arrangements

   Practice separately:

   rhythm parts

   lead vocal

   vocal harmonies

2. Work on Beatles Medley ("She Loves You"/"I'll Follow the Sun"/ "Twist and Shout")

   Practice separately:

   rhythm parts

   lead vocal

   vocal harmonies

3. Review new songs learned at last rehearsal ("Lawdy, Miss Claudy"/"Heartbreak Hotel")

   Run-through 3 times

Break

4. Review complete set list

THE BASIC COMPONENTS

Rhythm parts

The rhythm parts should be carefully constructed. Bass, drums, and rhythm guitar should work together until they have built a basic accompaniment that's interesting and effective. One of the problems that plague inexperienced bands is getting these particular instrumentalists to work closely together. Too many bass players prefer "lead"-style runs and flourishes, forgetting to nail down the bottom. The result is a weak overall sound. Drummers tend to be better about holding down the basic rhythm pattern, but often they change phrases in midstream, catching the bass and rhythm guitar players by surprise.

As for rhythm guitar players, their greatest failing is insufficient awareness of how important their role is. There is an art to playing rhythm guitar. It involves learning to pick and damp in such a way that you are exploiting the rhythmic and percussive potential of the electric guitar, as well as just playing chords. You must also work closely with bass and drums, something many rhythm guitar players don't bother to do.

Listen to a fine professional rhythm section—John Mellancamp, Tom Petty, the Rolling Stones. Notice how consistent and simple their playing is, and how well they play *together*. No one is showing off; the bottom line is the beat, pure and simple. That's what you want to strive for.

Lead parts

Once it has been decided where lead breaks will go and what the chord changes will be in these sections, lead players must come up with good leads as soon as possible. Don't put it off; the leads will just pile up on you. This should be done on your own time; composing a lead break that is interesting and durable can be slow work, and it's a waste of band time to do it in the middle of a rehearsal.

Double lead work, where two guitars, say, share the lead in harmony with each other, can be appealing in the course of an arrangement—here's where rehearsal time can be put to good use.

Lead fills should be more than just arbitrary. Where do the musical ideas come from? Start with the song itself. Improvise a melodic line that fits the basic chord changes. Take the song's main theme and play variations on it. Don't just blast notes at random; always try to think of something interesting that relates to what the other instruments are doing: echo the basic rhythm pattern, for instance, and build a lead on it. As for chops, get out your favorite CDs and tapes, listen to the leads you like, and try to determine *why* you like them; then go for that quality as you create your own leads. Once you have developed a lead you like, don't stop there; you should be able to play it in your sleep!

Vocals

Backup vocals are often neglected. Band members usually think, "We'll add some harmonies later." This is a trap you should avoid. Get into the habit of arranging your backup vocals at the same time you're arranging the instrumental parts. Good strong harmonies will give you a commercial appeal that is impossible to overemphasize. Club owners, agents, and promoters respond to this; it's one of the first things they look for. It will make you a more valuable band.

Often you'll want to work around a piano, or with just an acoustic guitar, to find and set your vocal parts. Once you've done this, go right to full instrumentation, at full volume. Suddenly, of course, you won't be able to hear yourself or find your notes, and your fingers will get lost as you try to sing and play at the same time. Well, what did you expect? Just keep it up until everything's happening smoothly again. This awkward stage is absolutely necessary. If you can't do it in performance conditions, *you can't do it.*

Basic Musical Components of a Band

- Rhythm section:

  drums

  bass

  rhythm guitar
- Lead instruments:

  lead guitar

keyboards

solo horns

- Vocals

lead singer

backup singers (harmony)

REHEARSAL TOOLS

There are two indispensable rehearsal tools that every band should have. One of them is the tape recorder. Use it! Just like a coach watching the films of the previous week's game, you'll learn amazing things when you listen to a playback of something you've just performed. All the weaknesses and holes are there; you'll hear them with a finality that'll bowl you over. Good things, too, that you hadn't really noticed will jump out at you.

A simple, permanent setup is what you want. It doesn't have to be expensive; a standard cassette recorder will do, but make it stereo if possible—you'll hear more details that way. Hang your mikes and leave them; set up playback speakers and leave them. The system has to be accessible at a moment's notice or else—human nature being what it is—you'll rarely make good use of it.

The other valuable tool is a metronome. Get a loud one, if you can afford it, with a strobe-light feature. If not, mike a cheap one and put it through an amplifier channel. What the metronome does best is help resolve arguments over tempo (time), which can get bloody. I once worked with a drummer who dragged up-tempo numbers and sped up ballads. A drummer who is guilty of those particular sins should probably prepare to make a living flipping burgers—but this drummer had a problem even *perceiving* the problem! We proved it to him by dragging in a kid who owned a metronome and running tests. His first response (one common to musicians with erratic time when they first face the machine) was to swear the metronome was veering off the beat. But he made his peace with the device and eventually developed into a steady drummer.

PLAY OUT AS SOON AS YOU CAN

While you're in the preparation period, always keep your eyes open for a chance to sneak preview your act in public—as informally as possible. There is plenty of work for bands who don't mind playing for nothing. You can take advantage of this opportunity, even if you've prepared only a few numbers, by performing for street fairs, benefits, outdoor rallies, and free park events. No pressure, no money, just a chance to fall on your face (*or* blow the crowd away) and go back to the rehearsal studio with a new understanding of what has to be done.

SET YOUR GOALS AND KEEP REVISING THEM

Your first goal is simply to complete the preparation stage and begin to get work. But that will happen. And then you'll need a new short-range goal. What'll it be? You might as well think about it up front and call it, for now, a medium-range goal. And while you're at it, go ahead and define a long-range goal. Because without clear goals, your progress is apt to be erratic and misguided.

I knew some musicians in a band that seemed to be headed for a recording contract and concert work. Yet instead of developing their original material, they amazed everyone by booking out in long strings of club and resort engagements where they were required to play mostly covers of Top-40 material. The best musicians left the band one by one, and although this group still exists, it's no longer considered a contender for national attention. The members of this band did not set clear goals for themselves. Somewhere in their minds was something vague and unclear, resembling a goal ("We want to make it!") but it wasn't clear enough ("We want to be doing a 50 percent original show by spring") to affect their everyday choices.

So a good band fell into oblivion. They failed to survive because they made stupid booking decisions, which choked their creative development. If their goals had been sensible and clearly stated, their decision-making would have followed from these goals and it would have been harder to be so self-destructive.

Your first goals are easy because they are automatically clear: get work—*any* work; gross over $1,500 a week. Later, when these initial goals have been achieved, the process of setting goals becomes subtler and puts a greater demand on your imagination. Goals in the middle stages of a band's development are a bit more difficult to articulate; you have to work harder at it. This is why it is important to form the habit of setting goals at the very beginning. Always have clearly defined (1) short-range, (2) medium-range, and (3) long-range goals. They must be clear. And as you achieve them, you must keep coming up with new ones. That's right, it never stops—unless you do. Some people have an instinct for goals, others have to make themselves think about it. Don't leave it to chance.

Sample Goals for a Working Band

Short-Range Goals

> Get a paying gig!
> Play as many free gigs as possible for practice
> Work at least one night a week in the immediate area
> Rehearse at least one time a week
> Learn five new songs a month
> Make a reasonable audition tape

Medium-Range Goals

> Work at least three nights a week
> Turn down poor paying gigs whenever possible; stop playing freebies
> Perform at least two original songs per show
> Make a high-quality recording for sale at shows
> Break into the regional market beyond hometown gigs

Long-Term Goals

> Work only venues seating over 250 people
> Get a recording contract
> Perform only original material
> Break out of the regional market; play a national tour
> Play at least one major industry showcase

THE FIRST GIG

You'll have to scramble and wait for your first paying gigs. If some of the band members have been in other local working bands (with good reputations) that's good; it will provide contacts with club owners and agents that might get you work right away. But if you're a brand-new band, you'll have to work harder at booking now than you ever will again. You *can* break through without tremendous difficulty if you follow the right procedure. First you'll need a basic booking kit.

Pictures

One 8 × 10-inch, black-and-white glossy—of the band, naturally. Take it to a printer and have 500 copies run off. Have your name (the band should have a name by now!), mailing address, and telephone number printed on the bottom border.

CONTACT: CROWS NEST

<u>CROWS NEST</u>
Joan DeSimone — lead vocals
Paul DeSimone — lead guitar, vocals
Bill Henderson — rhythm and slide guitar, electric violin
Doug Booth — bass, lead vocals
Steven Grimley — drums

—Repertoire—

Songs: Recorded by:

Songs:	Recorded by:
AFTER MIDNIGHT	Eric Clapton
BACK TO CALIFORNIA	Carol King
BLUE SUEDE SHOES	Elvis Presley, Carl Perkins
BOTTLE OF RED WINE	Eric Clapton
BROWN SUGAR	Rolling Stones
COLD RAIN AND SNOW	Grateful Dead
DANCING IN THE STREET	Shirelles, Mamas & Papas
FEELIN' ALL RIGHT	Traffic, Joe Cocker
FOR WHAT IT'S WORTH	Buffalo Springfield
HAPPY	Rolling Stones
HOME TO YOU	Seatrain
HONKY TONK WOMEN	Rolling Stones
IT'S TOO LATE	Carol King
JUMPING JACK FLASH	Rolling Stones
KEEP ON GROWING	Eric Clapton
LET IT RAIN	Eric Clapton
LET THE SUN SHINE	Hair
MIDNIGHT SPECIAL	Creedence Clearwater Revival
MORNING DEW	Grateful Dead
MULESKINNER BLUES	Dolly Partin
ONLY YOU KNOW AND I KNOW	Dave Mason, Delaney & Bonnie
PROUD MARY	Creedence Clearwater Revival
SMACKWATER JACK	Carol King
STORMY MONDAY BLUES	Allman Brothers, Bobby Bland
SUMMERTIME	Janis Joplin
SWEET SWEET MUSIC	Original
TRY A LITTLE TENDERNESS	Otis Redding, Three Dog Night
WILD HORSES	Rolling Stones
WILD NIGHT	Van Morrison
WILL YOU STILL LOVE ME TOMORROW	Carol King, Shirelles

— Available for nightclubs, parties, dances and concerts.

Rep (repertoire) sheet

This is a single sheet of white paper on which is printed (1) the names and instruments of all members of the band; (2) a list of the material you can perform, including the artist who originally recorded it (pad this out if you have to; you should list at least twenty-five songs); (3) mailing address and telephone; and, at the bottom, (4) some statement like "Available for concerts, clubs, dances, and parties." The print must be immaculate; have it laser-printed if possible. Make up a hundred or so photocopies.

Tape

On the recording system that you've been using at rehearsals, make a representative demo tape. If your rehearsal system doesn't make the grade, find someone with an amateur home studio. A reasonable home studio should have a quiet, well-padded room, some decent mikes and stands, an inexpensive 8-channel mixing board, and one of the numerous sophisticated, reasonably priced 4-track recorders that are now available.

Record your four or five strongest numbers and mix them down to a stereo "master." Cut out the false starts and long pauses, and then have a dozen or so cassette copies made up. Try to get a friend to do the dubbing for nothing, but listen to each cassette carefully. If there's a sharp drop in quality between the master and the copies, say thanks a lot, and take them elsewhere.

Basic supplies

You'll need 9 × 12-inch heavy manila envelopes (to package your photo, rep sheet, and tape), an address book, and a wall calendar to hang by your phone.

You now have your basic booking kit. You're ready to go out and start hustling.

Begin by taking the kit around to every club you know that books bands. There may be some you don't know of; check newspaper ads and listings. (Don't even talk to agents at this point—not unless they already know some of you personally and have a genuine interest in the band.) Hit the club at closing time, because the manager and possibly the owner will be there then, counting the money. Introduce yourselves, inquire about open dates, and leave a picture and a rep sheet. Tell them you have a tape if they're interested, but don't give it to them unless they specifically request it. Thank them for their time and leave—they're busy.

Go somewhere else and do the same thing.

When you've covered all the clubs, start following up. Make the rounds again. Through your persistence, club owners' raw curiosity may be aroused; after all, you appear businesslike, which is more than they can say for most of the bands who approach them. They'll probably ask you where you've worked. Don't lie, but make it sound as good as possible. If you haven't worked legitimately, offer to audition. Club owners like to have audition bands (they're free) for slow nights, and will probably schedule you.

Later on in your career free auditions will be something you just don't do, but for now—take the work. And be sure to confirm, both by mail (send a letter repeating the details you agreed on) and a couple of times by phone—especially a day or so before the gig.

Club owners are notorious for having holes in their heads, and to make matters worse, they treat audition bands with cavalier indifference. One of my old bands showed up at a club to audition and found another band set up on stage. Our original agreement had been made five weeks earlier and no one had bothered to confirm it. The club owner, meanwhile, had forgotten all about it and only dimly remembered that we existed at all.

On audition night, with everything set, make sure every friend you ever had is there, ready to boogie. The display of a substantial following weighs heavily in your favor. When it's over, have a talk with the club owner. Ask for a legitimate engagement (two or more nights). You should have found out beforehand what the club offers bands the first time around. Don't settle for less—unless there's a very good reason. Shake the owner's hand. Presto, you're a working band.

Soon this first gig will grow into a steady booking operation. That's what chapter 3 is about.

3

HOW TO RUN YOUR OWN BOOKING OPERATION

ooking is the absolute lifeblood of your business enterprise. I've seen good bands who weren't working, and when I asked them why, *they didn't know*. Don't let this happen to you. In the case of most of these bands, nobody was minding the store. Either an agent had told them he would keep them working, then forgot about it while the band retired to their phones to wait for a call, or they were being "managed" by someone who was too lazy or inept to get out of bed in the morning.

Take responsibility for your own destiny—take it into your own hands—because if you don't, no one else will, unless they intend to take advantage of you. Does this sound paranoid? Well, a touch of paranoia is not out of place in this business. It's a healthy sign, unfortunately (shark-filled waters and all that).

Don't worry too much about your first gig. It will come. Clubs are always looking for new faces, and sooner or later destiny's finger will point to yours. You'll want to work everywhere you can for a while; you've got to be seen. Every time you work, it's a showcase for more work. Take advantage of this; when you have an engagement, make sure you alert other club owners and invite them over to take a look at you.

Don't bother to approach agents at this time. They're not interested in brand new bands; they don't have to be. Just concentrate on doing a good job of building and expanding your bookings and let word of your band reach them on its own. It will. Meanwhile, take care of daily business. Your goal at this stage should be to reach a point where you're always booked one month ahead. In other words, if today is September 1, you should have September fully booked and be arranging your October bookings.

AGGRESSIVE BOOKING TECHNIQUES

The essence of good booking is a combination of aggressiveness and attention to detail. You must initiate contacts and you must follow up on them. Don't make the mistake of depending on others. Even with the best and kindest intentions they will let you down. You can't give other people credit for too much presence of mind. Sometimes they surprise you, but more often than not you must take care of business on your own.

Don't rely on unspoken assumptions because you assumed things were "understood." If a club owner from out of town approaches you at a gig and wants to hire you, give out your card—but get his or her name and number and follow up on it yourself. Don't wait for a call. For any number of reasons the owner may just never get around to making that call; the contact may go nowhere if you don't take the initiative.

If a club owner hires you, make sure all details are spelled out. Unscrupulous club owners will take advantage of you in a heartbeat; they'll use your own vagueness or reticence against you. Don't shake hands until you've agreed on (1) date, (2) starting and quitting time, (3) number of sets, and (4) exact amount and form of payment. As soon as you get home, send him a letter of agreement restating every detail.

It's not that all club owners are evil. But they have come up through a business in which muscle counts. The strong survive and the weak get muscled; if you appear weak, they're apt to take a cheap shot at you out of mere habit. To the few trustworthy club owners I've known, apologies—but you know even better than I do that what I'm saying is true.

As for the band, you'll find it wise always to do honest business. Club owners may try to screw you, but don't ever try to screw them. They can hurt you in too many ways. The way to win respect is to deal with everyone firmly and honestly. If your booking operation is energetic, clean, and businesslike, the word will get around and result in more and better work. Nothing could be worse for you than to earn a reputation as undependable.

Booking Checklist

Approach club owners personally. Meet them. Put your material directly in their hands.

Follow up on the initial contact. Don't wait by the phone, hoping it will ring; make the call yourself.

When you get a booking, make sure the details—date, time, money, number of sets, etc.—are spelled out.

Send a confirmation letter, restating the details. Keep a copy for your files.

Use the phone

You can do lots of business without going any farther than your phone. Before you pay a visit to a club, for example, you can find out who's who by a quick chat with the day bartender. Almost everybody can either be reached by phone, or their whereabouts narrowed down by means of this instrument.

Keep trying; most people in the music business will not return your calls if they don't know you. You can leave messages until you're blue in the face! The worst possible thing to do is wait, day after day, for the return call. If your call hasn't been returned in twenty-four hours, it won't be. Make it a rule to leave your name and number and then call back *the same day* if your call isn't promptly answered.

Make all your calls between 10 A.M. and 1 P.M. and all your follow-ups before 5:00 the same day. You'll be amazed how that simple rule smooths your telephone communications.

Confirm by mail

If an agreement on terms—or an understanding of any sort—is made by phone, mail a letter as soon as you hang up, restating those terms, and keep a copy. Two months later when the owner says, "We never agreed to" this point or that point, you simply wave your copy of the letter. If the owner has a reputation for stiffing bands, you may want to send the letter by *certified mail*; that way you'll have proof that it was received.

Personal visits can lead to work

Sometimes a personal visit to a club owner is preferable to a phone call. Many of them drift in and out of their clubs so often during the day that no one knows where they are at any given moment. During evening business hours (prime time for noise) it's almost impossible to talk over the phone; the club owner can't hear what you're saying, and distraction can lead to irritation—at you. Show up at closing time. The owner will almost certainly be there then.

BOOKING COLLEGES

One of the most effective things you can do is take a day to visit a university or college campus. Small colleges don't require a full day, but the big universities do. The whole band should participate in a commando booking raid, and the visit should be planned carefully.

One or two of you can cover the campus with publicity materials (flyers, posters, pictures) while others go from dorm to dorm, fraternity to fraternity, or sorority to sorority. Wherever you go, talk to people. Is the social chairperson around? If not, get a name and the phone number of the frat or dorm floor. Find out what bands have worked there before. Were they booked through an agent? Which one? And so on.

Somebody should go to the student union. Find out who books the bands for mixers, dances, or the campus tavern. Scan the bulletin boards where upcoming social activities are advertised. Which organizations are presenting bands? Drop by their offices and find out what's cooking in the near future, and who hires the bands.

Leave pictures and publicity materials with all these people. Even if nobody hires you on the spot, you've laid some groundwork. You've gotten your name around, and you've found out exactly who to call for work, all over the campus. Follow up these contacts, and check with them at regular intervals—you're bound to get a gig there sooner or later, and from that point on, one thing will lead to another. Multiply this by all the campuses in your area and you have a formidable source of work—and one that's usually available only through booking agents (because most bands are too lazy to do what you're doing)!

Checklist for University Bookings

- Flyers, posters, pictures, your sample tape. Don't leave home without them!

- Fraternities, sororities, dormitories: ask who books the entertainment for their events.

- Student union: find out who books the campus tavern, the student union-sponsored dancers, mixers, and parties.

- Bulletin boards: check out the names of other campus organizations who present live entertainment events.

HOW TO SET YOUR PRICE AND MOVE IT UP

All the $50,000-a-night bands love to tell nostalgic stories about being paid $35 a night for their first humble gigs. You might as well go ahead and work for peanuts, too, to establish your own myth. It's okay; just don't do it more than once or twice. If it gets around that you can be had cheap, you will be, rest assured. So even though you might *settle* for less, never *ask* for less than $200. Don't be shy. Always talk about money up front; don't make it an afterthought. Speak right up; it saves time.

In the long run your goal is to work your way up to a standard price below which you will not go, barring the most unique circumstances. The day will come when you must turn down $200 because you've decided never to go under $250. It's tricky, and you will meet resistance at every stage, even, ironically, from agents, who may want you to remain cheap so they can sell you effortlessly.

Nightclubs pay the same for nonunion bands now as they did years ago. Club owners hardly have a right to ask four or five musicians to put in a full night's work for less than $50 a person—but they do it. And they'd get you for a wooden nickel if they could. So stand your ground. Once you've proved yourselves and are no longer an audition band, set a bottom limit for your services and don't go below it.

Be aware of what the clubs pay other bands. Ask around. If the situation is in doubt, ask for twenty-five to fifty dollars more per night than you'll take, and work your way down from there. No matter what figure you demand, they'll try to haggle you down, so you might as well start high.

Keep in mind that college organizations have more money to spend. They're not squinting at profit-and-loss statements as are club owners. They start the year with money in their budget and it's their job to spend it. For college one-nighters, ask seventy-five to a hundred dollars more than you'll take.

Be realistic. Try to figure out if a low offer is justified by an off-setting publicity or prestige factor. Haggle a bit, but have a feeling for the club's or organization's *real* position. Know when to stop haggling. And don't lie about what you've been paid elsewhere. You can't get away with it; club owners all talk to one another and so do college social chairpersons; they know what you've been paid. What you have to do is convince them you're worth more and you're not going to take less.

Don't stand still. Always be pushing that average figure up. When you're in a club, look for feedback that can help you make a case for a raise. Check with the waitresses: How are tips? Check with the bartenders: How's business at the bar? See if you can find out what the cash-register tape reads at the end of the night. If the club books you a second and a third time, you're due for a raise; try for $50 more per night.

Here's the rule: don't price yourself out of the market, but don't sell yourself short, either.

CONTRACTS CAN BE USEFUL TOOLS

First of all, you're not about to start hauling people into court for breach of contract. At this point you probably can't afford the time, the hassle, the legal charges, or the bad will. There will come a day when you make a mistake and let a floundering club owner stiff you for $2,500; that's when you'll go to court. You probably won't collect, but at least your signed contract will qualify you to join all the other bereaved creditors at the owner's financial wake (the bankruptcy proceedings!). Meanwhile, you can get good use out of a standard contract if you think of it as an instrument of understanding. In other words, here's a piece of paper, signed by both you and who-ever is retaining your services—tangible evidence that you've agreed on something. And the actual terms you've agreed on are written down on the same piece of paper. You have a copy, the owner has one, and—unless one of you hasn't signed it—there's no possibility of a misunderstanding.

In the ongoing war of nerves between you and those you work for, a signed contract gives you a little bit of muscle. You need it, too, because in most matters the owners have *all* the muscle. It's a buyer's market, and they're buying, so they have the upper hand, and they'll express it by trying to bamboozle you at the last minute. They'll claim you agreed to work for less than the figure you recall. Or they'll try to get more work out of you. Sometimes the misunder-standing is honest. If you can produce your copy of a signed contract in such a situation, you'll have more control of the outcome.

A band I was in was booked for several nights at a large ski resort club in Vermont. After we had arrived, the manager said he wanted us to do a special happy hour in conjunction with an annual cross-country race that was being held that week (a big deal for him). It wasn't in our contract (signed by both him and our agent), so we asked for extra pay. He refused, but said we ought to do it any-way because the booking agent had said that we would (that remark, clearly false, was allowed to pass in silence). We made it clear, politely, that we wouldn't play the extra show.

A few minutes before zero hour he drove up to the band house and said he'd pay us an extra $150 for one set. But by then it was too late; half the band was off skiing or out of town for the afternoon. He went away fuming. It seems he had told his boss, the owner, that it was all set, then lost face because he couldn't deliver.

The postscript to this tale is that our booking agent received a scathing letter from the boss saying we had wrecked the band house and he never wanted us back. Because we had cleaned up carefully before leaving, we could only conclude that the vindictive manager went in and roughed the place up to make us look bad. These are some of the people and practices you must expect to run into as a working band, so you'd better learn every possible means of self-defense.

Upon your verbal agreement, sign and send out two copies of the contract with all terms of agreement written in, including riders (special agreements not in your standard contract—like overnight accommodations or use of your equipment by another band). Here's a standard simple contract form that you can use or adapt for your own special requirements. Ask the other party to sign and return one copy to you. They may stall on getting it back to you, so don't wait till the last minute to begin pressing for it. Follow through by phone or with a visit. If an agent is in the middle, pester the agent. If he or she claims the club owner won't sign, suggest that if somebody doesn't work on it, you will call the club owner personally (and be prepared to do it).

Standard Sample Contract

THIS CONTRACT for the personal services of musicians, made the

_____ day of _____ 19_____, between

_____

(hereinafter called the "employer") and _____
(hereinafter called the "employees").

WITNESSETH, That the employer hires the employees as musicians severally on the terms and conditions below. The leader represents that the employees already designated have agreed to be bound by said terms and conditions. Each employee yet to be chosen shall be so bound by said terms and conditions upon agreeing to accept his employment. Each employee may enforce this agreement. The employees severally agree to render collectively to the employer services as musicians in the orchestra under the leadership of _____, as follows:

NAME AND PLACE OF
ENGAGEMENT _____

Date(s) of Employment _____

Hours of Employment _____

Type of Employment (specify whether dance, stage show, banquet, etc.)

_____

Wages Agreed Upon _____

To Be Paid _____

_____	_____
(Employer's name)	(Leader's name)

_____	_____
(Signature of employer)	(Signature of leader)

(Street)	(City)	(Street)	(City)

(State)	(Phone)	(State)	(Phone)

Never forget to bring your signed copy of the contract to a gig. Be ready to show it at any time. Often, when you arrive you'll be dealing with someone you never talked to before, who has erroneous information. Just quietly and affably insist on the provisions of the contract. These include starting time, quitting time, number of sets, price, and whatever else you consider important.

If, at the end of the night, you don't get the full sum you agreed to work for, make a quick choice between the alternatives: (1) take what you can get and run; or (2) don't take a cent, go away, and sue later. The only reason to chose the first alternative, in my opinion, would be in a case where your arm will be broken, or worse, if you continue to insist on your full amount. There are some types of characters you don't dare sue. These are the extremely heavy variety of mob-connected club owners you encounter occasionally. If they have a reputation for not paying up, just don't work for them in the first place and you'll never have the problem. Incidentally, if you *are* going to sue, don't take any money from the club. If you do, that will be construed in court as acceptance of partial payment and you will lose your case.

Your strongest weapon, should you ever want to fight, is the refusal to go on. Done properly, at the last possible minute, it can have a stunning effect. Money, previously nonexistent, suddenly appears. If, for instance, you finish the first night of a two-night engagement and are not paid because business was slow, reply pleasantly that you'll expect to have your money before going on the following night. If it's not there, don't go on. You'd get nothing for the second night either, so at least you've saved yourself another night's unpaid labor. If the money does exist, you'll get it quickly. But don't expect the club owner to be nice about it, because what you've just done is administer a well-deserved smack on the wrist.

Here's another, more complicated situation. A band I played with was opening for a '50s rock 'n' roll star at a large motor inn. The show was being backed by a union local and promoted by an agent whom we knew to be erratic (we decided to take the risk). The star, it happened, didn't carry his own sound system, and the agent made no attempt to rent one for him and his band. Instead it was assumed that we would take care of it. We agreed to handle his sound—considerable extra work for our roadie—if we were compensated for it. Sure, sure, they said. We had it attached to the contract in a rider.

When the first night's show ended, we were paid, but the extra money wasn't there. The agent said we'd get the whole thing on the following night. The next day we made it clear we weren't going on—and the star would be without a sound system—if we weren't paid the extra sum before show time. But nobody seemed to hear us.

When eight o'clock came we were upstairs, seven blocks of granite. The house manager called up, frantic: "Get the hell on stage! Do you realize it's after eight?" Our roadie went down to the lobby to explain the situation. A very large union official was there, making threatening noises, but our roadie was himself large enough to deal with it and simply stood his ground. Finally, in disgust, the union man went to the safe and gave us the money, to be subtracted from the agent's commission. We said thank you and went on.

Scenes like this should not occur often. But be psychologically prepared for them when they do. And if you've decided to use your ultimate weapon, make sure not to waffle. Once you've committed yourself, don't budge.

There will be gigs where a contract seems unnecessary. You know the club owner personally, or you worked without a contract before, so why start now, and so on. Judgment is the key to these situations; don't ruin an otherwise decent situation by blindly refusing to make an exception.

Occasionally you will encounter a club owner who refuses to have anything at all to do with contracts, for personal reasons. We worked many times for a club owner in New York City without a contract. When I asked him to sign one "for our tax records," he became very testy and walked off in the opposite direction. But this man was absolutely honest and fair, and had never misled us or taken advantage of us in any way. What the hell; I just filed a contract without his signature and forgot the whole thing.

That experience is not typical, however. Typically the rule is: if it's not in the contract, it never happened. So get some contract forms printed up and start using them.

4

IMAGES AND AGENTS

T he secret of effective publicity and promotion is to understand how information moves in your area. How do the people you want to reach find out what's going on? What radio stations do they listen to? What newspapers do they read? Which form of media are they most likely to check for entertainment information?

Information patterns are different from one city to another, and you should be conscious of the pattern that relates to your needs. Otherwise you will be putting up posters in places where nobody goes, missing media deadlines, and wasting press kits on the wrong people.

HOW TO DO YOUR OWN
PUBLICITY AND PROMOTION

Promoting yourself consists almost entirely of publicizing your name. This appears to be such a bald truth that I'll expand on it. You will discover, as you become better and better known in your region, that 75 to 80 percent of those who have heard of your band, who mention you to others and accept you as fully established local stars, have never actually seen your band perform! The ironic conclusion must be drawn that for your name to appear *in certain places* legitimizes you in a way no amount of ordinary local appearances can. If you're included in the promotion for a "Big Event," for instance, it has an amazing effect on your reputation.

I worked in a bar band that had appeared around town steadily for over a year, but we didn't cross the line to become regional "celebrities" until we opened a concert for a nationally famous band (bookings picked up immediately). Thousands of dollars had been spent on radio and newspaper promotion, and the concert was a sellout in the city's big sports arena. *We* didn't sell it out, of course; *they* did. But for two or three weeks our name was everywhere, visibly and audibly. Our (privately pressed) EP was all over the airwaves, because local announcers thought it was fun that we were doing such a big show and decided to help push us. One thing does lead to another. Suddenly we were well known by God knows how many people who had never actually seen us perform—and perhaps never would.

You don't have to appear in Madison Square Garden to create this effect for your band in a modest fashion. Working in clubs will get your name displayed in the press and elsewhere, because clubs often advertise your appearance. This is absolutely free exposure for you; you don't pay a cent.

You should explore all possible ways of publicizing yourselves for nothing before you begin spending money. Most radio stations and newspapers have free entertainment listings, as do local entertainment guides, the "what's happening?" type of giveaway that you find in drugstores and supermarkets. Use them. Type up your schedule for the next two weeks and send it to the person who compiles the listings. Call first and find out (1) that person's name, and (2) how far in advance the information must be received.

From this point on, your promotional operation will require an outlay of cash—*how much* cash depends on you. If you're sitting on vast capital reserves and you can burn them up fast . . . rent a billboard! Have your name sky-written over the beach on the Fourth of July! A new radio station in Texas had a grand piano dropped by a hovering helicopter into a stadium of onlookers, merely to publicize their opening day. If you've got the bread, don't think small!

Chances are, however, you'd prefer to ease into the PR game and start with a more modest approach. Remember that whatever money you drop here is well spent if it results in work—one $300-gig more than compensates for $200 spent on promotion. Be thrifty, but don't be cheap. To those who've never seen you, you *are* your publicity; if it's cheesy, you'll be thought of as a cheesy band. The better the approach, the more work you'll get.

Publicity Outlet Checklist

1. Local newspapers: "What's Happening/Calendar" listings, music editor, local news editors
2. Local radio stations: calendar, talk show, music producers
3. College newspaper/radio as above

4. Local cable companies (bulletin board listings)

5. Local arts councils (listing services, etc.)

Press kit

You have the basics already, your rep sheet and your picture. I should emphasize that the picture is *very* important; you must have a good one. It's the cornerstone of your publicity. It will be used again and again, reproduced in all possible media situations. If it's boring, pretentious, or painfully awkward, you'll regret it. Have it done by a proven photographer. A friend, if possible, but no amateurs: they'll only waste your time. Most important, you should take it seriously.

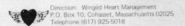

Direction: Wingèd Heart Management
P.O. Box 10, Cohasset, Massachusetts 02025
Telephone (617) 925-5018

John Lincoln Wright — lead vocals and songwriter. Former lead vocalist of the Beacon Street Union and Eagle. John has been on the Boston music scene for nearly 10 years, during which his bands have recorded 3 LP's, 10 singles, and rolled up a considerable amount of national touring experience. A songwriter and singer noted for his strong vocal style and performing skill.

John Macy — pedal steel guitar. Played in house bands along the "89ers Strip" Lubbock, Texas. In the Boston area, with Jeff Thompson, Steve Whynot and Country Kitchen.

Ed Hughes — drums, vocals. Boston area rock bands, including Apogee. Former stage manager, the Boston Teaparty.

John McDonald — lead guitar, vocals. Boston rock groups, including Indescribably Delicious. Guitar and banjo in folk coffeehouses, such as the Nameless, in Harvard Square.

Ray Jacques — bass guitar, vocals. Rock & roll bands in Maine and Boston. Tidal Waves, Tunerville Trolley, Jar.

Bill Henderson — electric fiddle. Guitar and fiddle with Shaft (New York City) and Crows Nest (Boston). Studio work, New York City.

"...the baddest bunch of pickers around"

Don't be macho about it and refuse to primp. Go ahead—look loose, informal, enhanced, mythic. Think and talk about what to wear. Use the occasion to discuss your feelings about a collective image. Make your appearance support that image.

Buy a stack of folders, the kind with inside pockets that are used to hold loose papers. Have your band's name printed on the front of the folder and slip your picture, rep sheet, and any other relevant publicity into the pockets. You should include photocopies of all published press reviews, impressive ads, and articles of any kind that mention your name favorably. For mailing, you'll need heavy manila (9 × 12-inch) envelopes.

Some bands like to have self-contained brochures or leaflets printed. I believe it's more important to have a press kit first—something flexible to which you can add or subtract items. If your personnel changes, or you suddenly acquire better press or improved status, a brochure has to be discarded and done over, but you can simply change the contents of the press kit. A demo cassette can also be stuffed into one of the pockets if desired.

The press kit has a million uses; it's your way of presenting yourself to those who can't meet you in person. Always keep some with you, although beware of fans who are after keepsakes or collector's items. Use the kits for business only, or you'll never be able to keep any around!

Sample press release

The reporters who compile entertainment news and gossip for local papers are hardworking human beings just like you and me. Anything you can do to make their jobs easier will reap rewards for you. A breezy, entertaining, informative press release like the following can supply them with ready-made copy. Try to mail (or e-mail) one of these out every month or so (or enlist a fan to do it), covering the area dailies, alternative weeklies, and regional entertainment tabloids.

FOR IMMEDIATE RELEASE
CONTACT: SUSAN KELLY, PRESS REP
(555) 555-1212
POKER FACE: CATCH 'EM WHILE YOU CAN

Look out for Poker Face! The Boston-based alternative country-rockers are breaking into the open after getting hotter and hotter for the past eighteen months. Word is that you'll only be able to see them at places like Great Woods a year from now, but luckily for the Boston area, "The Face" won't be hitting the concert trail immediately. As a result, what we have now is one of those rare moments in a band's history when they're just shy of becoming a "national act," yet you can still see them under casual conditions. So better not put it off. Poker Face is growing into a monster, and you can't keep a good monster down!

Jonny Lipsky is the band's local yokel focal point. A growly outlaw type, he does the lead singing and writes most of the band's original material. "Howl" Crowther, lead guitar, does some singing and writing, and so does "the Big Mac," Billy McCranor, slide guitar and atomic violin. The other band members include George Heath, acoustic guitar, John Macy, pedal steel, and Dave Kinsman, drums.

The band's sound is high-energy country, but with songs that echo urban insanity and angst (cross Henry Rollins with Travis Tritt, throw in equal amounts of Soundgarden and the Eagles, and you've got it). This is one of the tightest and most exiting bands to emerge in the area for a long time. Catch 'em this month at the Mid East, Johnny D's, and The Paradise—before they run away from home.

Display items

Find a printer who is relatively inexpensive and small enough to talk to customers. Take some time to chat about what you have in mind; listen to his or her advice. A good printer should be concerned about how to do what you want done. If you seem to be getting put down because you don't know printers' language, or if there's little interest in your ideas, take your work somewhere else. These are some of the items you should ask the printer to help you design and produce.

POSTERS

Print them on heavy poster stock, about 13 x 17 inches. The picture area should consist of the band's photograph and name in prominent, bold letters. Leave blank spaces at the bottom for whatever specific details you want to include: day, date, time. These can be added with magic marker or taken to your printer and run off inexpensively on the existing poster.

FLYERS

Occasionally there is a special club date or concert you want to promote heavily. You can have flyers reproduced cheaply on plain 8 × 10-inch paper stock, to be handed out or mounted on walls all over town. The mounting should be done with tape; if you use paste they'll stick forever, compounding the problem of urban glut (there are limits to zeal). Use masking tape and go to environmental heaven when you die.

BROCHURES OR LEAFLETS

As mentioned above, these are decidedly a luxury item. Some bands keep a stack of them on a table near the entrance door. Most of them seem to end up on the street or in the gutter.

BANNER OR TRAVELING EMBLEM

These valuable display items give your name maximum exposure for the money. A good-sized banner, with your name emblazoned on it in large letters, should be hung from the wall behind the band. That way, walk-ins will know immediately who you are. Merely to display your name attractively, to dispel anonymity, is to make your band appear more formidable and substantial on stage!

A traveling emblem is simply a logo (your name, specially designed, like a trademark) painted on the van or truck you use for band transportation. Wherever it goes, people in the street will notice your name. If it's someone's personal vehicle, all the better—the more it's out and around, the more name recognition you'll be getting. Just make sure whoever executes the job does it well. It should look like a professional sign-painting job, whether it is or not.

Specialty items

These promotional sundries are fun if you can afford to front some money for them. You'll be able to get a lot of it back because these items can be sold for profit, at your gigs or elsewhere. T-shirts, for example, with your logo silk-screened on the front, can be manufactured in bulk (try a few hundred at a time) for as low as $2.50 to $3 per shirt and sold for $8 or $10, depending on how greedy you are. The same principle holds for bumper stickers and buttons.

These are all effective publicity for you. Just make sure they're not ugly. And if you sell them, try and keep the price low. Don't lose sight of the point of the whole venture—to get as many of these items as possible out on the street!

Some unusual specialty items

There are many outlets for promotional items, usually listed in your local yellow pages; you pay a little more to work with them rather than directly with a printer, but their catalogs often give you clever ideas and they do have access to some unusual items. Some you might consider include (besides the popular T-shirt):

> keychains
> coffee cups
> bumper stickers
> pencils
> tote bags
> caps
> buttons

Office stuff

You'll need supplies, so you might as well go out and get them all at once. Letterhead stationery is a matter to discuss with your printer, who can also help you with business cards. You'll also find it handy to have picture postcards printed up, using the band's logo and official photograph. These have countless uses. There are many situations that call for a quick note to someone. A postcard is often more appropriate than a full-scale letter, and, once again, your picture and name will be brought to the recipients' attention. This is its real value—whether it's a thank-you note to a radio announcer who played your tape, a brief restatement of an agreement you just hatched on the phone, or just a hello to a club owner you haven't been in touch with lately, you're keeping your image bright and alive in these people's minds.

And this is exactly what you want to do always. If you do it well, and are consistent about it, large numbers of people will have heard all about you before they ever actually go out to see you.

HOW TO DEAL WITH AGENTS

One day, a booking agent will call. Don't relax. Agents have a way of introducing themselves to you with a flourish of promises. Do not assume they will now rush to take over all your booking responsibilities. They won't do that (unless you make a deal with them for exclusive representation—and that usually means management). What they will do is call you occasionally with a booking.

The fact that you've come to the attention of an agent is a mark of your progress. But you must continue to run your own booking operation—augmented by agents occasionally, perhaps even regularly, as you become better known outside of town—but always under your own control. This is important. Many a band drops the ball at this point and waits for the agent to call, rather than continuing to pursue bookings aggressively on its own. That's a mistake.

An "agent" can be anything from one lone individual working out of a private home to a whole office suite full of receptionists, secretaries, flunkies, junior agents, senior agents, and big wheels. As far as you're concerned, it amounts to the same thing: an agent is a connection between you and someone who might employ your band.

Agents are useful to you because (1) they are in touch with clubs and colleges beyond your range and can often get you a gig on the strength of their word alone, and (2) they sometimes have habitual or even exclusive booking arrangements with club owners and campus representatives that necessitate making deals through them alone.

If you get a gig through an agent, you must hand over 10 or 15 percent of your gross pay for services rendered. It's usually 15 percent for a one-nighter, 10 percent for a stretch of nights in a club. Good agents earn their commission on out-of-town one-nighters, but for local club dates they often do no more than you could easily do yourself.

By now you should have made some sort of contact with every club in your immediate area, and unless you've been told flatly, "We only book through the Dodo Agency," then you should be making your booking arrangements directly with the club owner. In fact, if you're trying to book a date in a certain club, don't even mention it to an agent—who will only say, "Oh, I can get you in there," then proceed to pick up the phone and make the deal before you do. Later you'll get a call: "Oh, I got you into the Blue Cockatoo." And there goes 10 percent you could have put into your own pocket.

Agents are like product distributors. You are the product and they are trying to "distribute" you to clubs and colleges in much the same way that a food distributor tries to sell soup to a grocery store. An agent, like a distributor, is always trying to nail down exclusive territory, and the simplest way to do this is to undersell all competitors, the other agents. An agent's line to a club owner is often something like: "I can get them for you cheaper," lowering your price to make the sale. Watch out for this. If an agent offers you a gig but the pay seems unaccountably slim, see if you can find out what's actually happening, perhaps by having an off-the-record chat with the source of the offer: the club owner or campus rep.

If you wonder why agents, who work for commissions, would want to push your price down rather than up, here's the answer: most agents make their big money on the bands they manage or book exclusively—not on independents like you. They concentrate most of their energy on promoting and booking their own bands and fighting to get top dollar for them. Your role is to be part of a stable of cheap bands that they can book easily at bargain rates and (most important) in volume. The way they look at it, it's a lot easier to keep ten bands working and netting regular income if they sell them cheaply.

This also is why you can't count on the average agency to be thinking about you all the time. Unless they have a piece of your management, they are apt to be somewhat negligent of your daily and weekly needs. You should not be depending on them for this kind of attention anyway. If you have occasional dealings with an agency, accept the fact that you'll have to take on a bit of the responsibility—and that means push them (gently), remind them of things, call *them*, don't wait for them to call you.

SOME QUESTIONS TO ASK AN AGENT

Before "signing on the dotted line" you should ask the agent at least some of the following questions:

> How many acts do you represent?
> What is the average fee you get for your acts?
> How long have you been in business?
> What services does your agency provide (contract negotiation; legal help; travel arrangements; PR advice)?
> Are there additional fees for additional services?
> Are you a member of any professional organizations?
> Can you give us as references the names of two bands you represent?
> Can you give us as references the names of two clubs who have worked with you ?

Now I come to a delicate point. Agents, in the course of their work, bend the truth a lot. Of course, the agents I know would be very angry to hear this because they don't think of themselves as liars; they regard themselves as professionals and strategists. From their point of view, concealing or altering information often merely makes their work easier and more effective. Conditions are always shifting under their own feet, yet their clients demand from them the illusion of permanence; this is bound to turn them into skeptics and falsehood artists. Most of their lies are small evasions and revisions. You ask them, "What's happening on the so-and-so gig?" They say, "I've been calling them every day but I can't get anything out of them." Translation: "Now that you mention it, maybe I'll give them a try."

Agents aren't the enemy, they're just busy, and the bulk of their business does not involve you. They are prone to neglect small details that loom large for you. Accommodations for an out-of-town gig, for example: "Oh yes, the club provides accommodations," they'll say, because they seem to remember that being the case. You arrive, however, and the club owner never heard of it. Little things like that will drive you crazy if you let them. Get in the habit of double-checking the details of all gigs (with the agent, or, if he or she is not available—and you believe it's important enough—with the club).

There are good agents and bad agents. The better an agent is, the more details will be handled capably. Some agents are simply sloppy and negligent. A band I was in was sent all the way to New Hampshire ski country in a snowstorm by an inefficient agent. When we pulled into the lodge, we saw the name of another band displayed on the marquee. The agent had booked *both* bands and neglected to cancel one of them. This agent had had an unsavory reputation around town for years.

The club owner, already sick of dealing with the man, provided us with accommodations and free drinks, and when we left the next day he gave us the agent's commission to cover our expenses and went on to bill the agent for our accommodations and bar tab. The agent never spoke to us again—and that's something you should be prepared for if you decide to retaliate, as we did. The agent will never deal with you again, and may try to slander you or otherwise sabotage your career. Be sure your name has a strong enough reputation to survive a cold war with a scorned agent.

And though it is sad to report, some agents can't resist falling into shady practices. I'll mention the most common one here, because it's often encountered by unsuspecting new bands. The agent will tell you your pay is, say, $300, minus 15 percent. At the end of the night the agent will be there to take the money, withhold the agency's cut, and hand you the rest in cash. What you don't know is that you were priced at $400 to the unsuspecting club owner, and the agent walks away with the extra $100. For this reason always insist on collecting your own fee and paying the agent's commission yourself. I need hardly add that an agent is much less likely to attempt this trick if the date is firmly contracted and the contracts signed by all parties.

Chapters 3 and 4 should have prepared you to start booking the band with confidence and efficiency. Just keep in mind this humbling thought: everyone is more powerful than you are at this stage of your career. It may not be true forever, but early in your career the band, like a child, is unknown, unsure, and vulnerable. People in the business can seem strange and harsh. But this won't always be true. Stick around. The more you work with them the less likely you are to be treated like a stranger. Before long you'll be able to do your wheeling and dealing with a confidence born of familiarity.

5

DEVELOPING A FOLLOWING

The quickest way to begin to be taken seriously is to demonstrate that you have a "following." Most simply, a following is a dependable and fairly sizable crowd of people who make a habit of coming out to see you. You need one. Very good bands have gone nowhere because they were unable to generate a loyal following. Your following is a signal to clubs and agents that you are beginning to arrive. To the agent, it means you are bookable; to the club owner, it means action—especially if your following is affluent and thirsty.

From your perspective, having a following means you'll never play to an empty house. This is comforting when you are going into a new room in a part of town where you are unknown; it's also a bargaining point with club owners and agents. Out of town it means you are the kind of band that can build a following. This is attractive to out-of-town club owners—it encourages them to take a chance on you the first time around in the hope that you'll be a solid draw on return engagements.

Quite frankly, there's no way you will initially generate a following without doing something exciting or fulfilling on stage. So don't expect it to happen automatically. You have to deserve it. And that means you have to make the people happy. How you do that is up to you. You can (1) be musically spectacular, (2) concentrate a lot of your work around home to give yourself a chance to snowball, and (3) get to know your fans—find out why they follow you, what you're doing right—and treat them well!

HAVE A HOME BASE

There's nothing like habit for building a following. Having a club where you can be found on a fairly habitual basis is an ideal situation early in your career. Try to find a well-situated club, where the regular patrons like you, and make an arrangement to work there on a weekly basis. Whether it's every weekend for a while, or regular early-week work (leaving you free to work elsewhere weekends) you should become associated in people's minds with that club—and the club, with you.

If a club is going to become your home base, it has to be a comfortable place for your following. The ambience of the club should not be hostile to their lifestyle or they won't show up. If your style (and theirs) is scruffy and down-home, the place shouldn't be a rap den, a hard-core haven, or a biker palace. The club regulars shouldn't be so different from your crowd that it causes trouble.

Other considerations are prices and dress code. If the cover charge and price of drinks are too steep for your following, they'll settle for seeing you only occasionally, but you want to have them there several nights a week. Dress codes are really a thing of the past in most rock clubs. But some of the fancier singles joints try to enforce "standards" and this could make for tension at the door. On the other hand, if your following is affluent and slick, this will never be a problem. Nor will money for drinks and cover, for that matter.

And speaking of money, remember that high pay should not be your prime objective in looking for a home-base club. Often the club is perfect, but can't afford yet to pay generously. That's fine: the habitual exposure is worth the difference, and if you build a following there, which is your prime objective, you'll soon be in a position to ask for more money (you'll be earning it for the club!).

Don't be surprised if, when you've doubled his or her business, the club owner still talks poor; that's to be expected. Keep your eye on the cash-register tapes and raise your price accordingly. Remember: you can always move your following to another club—and the owner knows it.

Home Club Checklist
Caters to your kind of people
Minimal cover charge; liberal free pass policy
Minimal dress code (or none)
Inexpensive drink and food prices
A casual booking pattern; leaving room for block booking your band on a regular basis, once you start drawing

FANS

Your fans don't mind telling you that you're important to them. Something the band is, or projects from the stage, makes them feel good. They like you, they like the scene around you—and in a sense they are the scene around you. Some fans come right up and make themselves known to you, others are less visible. You should learn to recognize them all and treat them cordially. Their continued and growing presence is crucial.

Core fans

These few hard-core followers will be your mainstay. They are the ones who will make you a significant part of their lives. You'll wonder if you deserve it, but they will have no doubts. They'll always be there and they'll turn new people on to you. Often they work or hang out in central locations, and are in daily touch with the folks you want to reach. They are your grapevine. Always let them know what's happening; keep them up to date on your schedule, changes of plan, and important appearances. Exchange phone numbers so that lines of communication are always ready to function. These fans especially deserve some extra attention from you. When you're in a club with a stiff cover charge, for example, make sure their names are on your guest list.

Out-of-town fans

As you begin to work farther and farther away from home, you'll want to build the same nucleus of fans in other places. After a few nights in a new club, you should know who your friends are. When you're due to return, these people can turn out more new fans. In the meantime, they should pester the club owner to get you back. Occasionally a fan can even help you set up other work in the area.

Gifts from fans

At one time, the members of a band I was in could eat full meals in three different "gourmet" restaurants for the price of a cup of coffee; we had generous discounts in two record stores, a department store, and a wine shop; and several bartenders around town rarely charged us for drinks. The way I saw it at the time was that here was a situation where a nice kind of symbiosis between the actual lives of the performers and the fans seemed to be functioning. We provided entertainment, which was what we had to offer, and they gave us food, drink, and in some cases, retail clothing—which was what they had to offer. A sentimental view, perhaps, but good memories to have, because, as you go up the ladder, life is never again so simple, and you are never again so close to your fans in a simple, down-to-earth relationship.

Fans enjoy doing favors for you, if they are in a position to do so; you'll discover that your fans are drawn from a fascinating array of businesses, crafts, trades, and even professions. You've probably got lawyers and accountants out there as well as waitresses, body-shop owners, photographers, bike-shop managers, record-store clerks, bartenders, printers, radio announcers, mechanics, astrologers, and God knows what. Whatever the case, you can make life easier on yourself, as well as more economical for the band, by getting to know your individual fans.

Fans and your ego

In general, you'll do well to keep your ego trimmed down to manageable proportions when relating to fans. They're nearly always friendly and supportive, but don't forget that even as they spoon out the ego food they are watching you very closely. They're sensitive to your feelings about them and can be easily turned off if you treat them in a high-handed or superior way.

It's easy to fall into the trap of acting like a Very Important Person, because that's how the fans treat you. Just remember: being in a band makes you no more important than when you were dishing up tacos for a living—which maybe you still are! After all, you are in a position to know what they don't know—that being on stage is only your job, not some exalted state of being that gives you a license for vanity, arrogance, and egomania.

Before leaving the pleasant subject of fans, I must strike a sour note. You will occasionally have fans who are just a drag. They are either distinctly disagreeable, in that their presence is boorish and brings everyone else down, or else they're violent and can hurt people. There's not much you can do about the harmless ones as long as they remain harmless. But if excessively unruly fans push you to a crisis point in your relations with the club or with your other fans, you may have to bar them from the places you play—awkward as that may be.

GROUPIES

I don't want to sensationalize this topic, except to say that hardly a musician exists—from Johann Strauss to Eddie Van Halen—who has not been burned at least once by a groupie. Not to say that groupies haven't been burned by musicians! But this book is biased: it reflects the musician's point of view. And so when it comes to groupies (I'll define that in a moment), the average musician should beware.

I apply the term "groupie" to both males and females. Groupies are obsessive fantasy seekers. Musicians are perfect fantasy objects—they project from the stage only a few carefully selected qualities; perhaps it's flash and cool, perhaps aggressiveness or studlike arrogance. It depends on what kind of show the band has chosen to put on.

But whatever the case, a musician's total personality, warts and all, does not come across; what does come across is a crafted theatrical image, and one that invites speculation: "Is she really like that?" "Mm, I wonder what he's like." Enough is left out of a stage image so that the groupie can complete it with fantasies; you thus become the walking, talking embodiment of these fantasies. The groupie mistakes the image for the total person, and is strongly attracted. Groupies can become so preoccupied with this process that music and musicians become their reason for being.

But you don't know that! What you know is that an extremely attractive person seems to have become attracted to *you.* Unwittingly, you may have hooked a shark. And just as a shark, once it knows it has been hooked, will indignantly snap your puny little line and take off, hook in mouth, groupies, once they are aware that there is more to you than first met their eye, will break off abruptly and cruise on in search of more fantasies. After all, most musicians live rather docile and unexciting lives offstage—they practice, they listen to music, they rehearse or jam—and somehow that's always a surprise to the groupie.

The real danger is that he or she will move on to someone else in your band, thus constellating all possible bad feelings: rejection, jealousy, hostility, and depression. A situation like that can invoke dissension in the band, clog up communications, and make it excruciating for you to work together. It can cause permanent damage to your relationship with the other band members—even break up the band.

Fans versus groupies

Groupies will use you as a necessary element of an exploitative psychological game they play with themselves, so you'll do well to steer a wide path around them—or at least understand that game before you walk into it. Fans, on the other hand, are willing and able to appreciate you fully without devouring you. They accept you for what you are. Be extra careful to treat your fans with respect and cordiality. You'll find a lifetime's worth of good and loyal friends among them.

BUILDING PR CONTACTS

PR (public relations) is part of your continuing effort to build up your following—only now you must become known to the people whose jobs place them in a position to help promote you favorably to a wider public. PR involves getting to know individuals who can do specific things for you.

Important PR contacts

1. The announcers for local radio stations who play music most similar to yours, or who are known to have an interest in local bands. As they jabber away on the air, they sometimes have occasion to put in a spontaneous plug.

2. The regional contributors ("stringers") for music publications like *Spin* or *Rolling Stone*. You never know when they're going to do a "survey" of "up-and-coming bands" in your area—or some such piece that could mention your name.

3. The local columnist who writes something called "The Music Scene" or "Club Notes"—a gossipy compendium of who's appearing where. These writers spend a lot of time "making the scene"—and they cherish their friendships with bands, so go get 'em.

4. Local freelance writers and reporters who like your music. They have access to the papers and they know how to write; they can therefore get you some press. Don't forget that a decent puff piece can always find publication somewhere—even if it's just the local throwaway entertainment guide. And once it's been printed somewhere, you have something for your press kit!

5. Record-store managers and salespeople. They talk about bands and music all day long to the record-buying public, as well as to other local and regional music people. They are also in regular touch with the merchandising and promotional staffs of the major record labels—who pick up much of their gossip and information from record stores.

6. Promo people for the major recording labels. They keep up to date on what's happening regionally because it's their job to promote records in the area. They file regular reports back to New York or L.A., and if they think a lot of you, they're liable to turn someone from their national A&R department on to you.

These people are the antennae in the music business. It is through them that you stand your best chance, in these early stages, of amplifying the news of your arrival. Make a point of finding out who they are and of striking up some sort of positive relationship with them.

Do some research. Talk to other musicians who've been around longer than you have. Make a list of good contacts. When you feel the band is ready, try to make a few personal connections. Introduce yourself casually and tactfully; do not come on with a stream of hype. Perhaps the individual in question has wandered into your home club. Make the contact straightforward and polite. Be sober, or you risk making an ass of yourself. A phone call is also a way of making the contact: extend an invitation to a gig. Or send one of your picture postcards—that's what they are for!

It's a good idea to compile a mailing list of music and media people with whom you want to keep in touch. Your key fans should also have a place on the mailing list, as should club owners, agents, and other musicians who have shown an interest in your music. Every now and then, get out a mailing.

Reasons to Send Out a Mailing

- When your schedule is set for the next two months, have it printed on the back of your picture postcard and send it out to those on the mailing list.

- When you're going to be involved in something special—an opening-act concert appearance that came through blind luck—let the people know, drop them a card.

- When you're returning to an out-of-town club, send out a notice to your fans in that town for solid word-of-mouth turnout to fill the place.

When a band builds a following, the process might appear to happen naturally. It just isn't true. Without a concerted effort, you will be lucky to have much of a following at all, outside of your circle of friends and those "naturals," your key fans. If you're going to be successful, you *must* push the boundaries of your following out among your own local version of a mass audience. And to do this takes imagination, initiative, strategy, and action.

6

CLUBS, COLLEGES, CONCERTS

T his book has had so much to say about clubs or bars that you'd think you wouldn't be able to find a working band anyplace else. Well, that's practically true. Today the bars are the launching pads for rock 'n' roll bands. Way back in the '60s, this was not the case: only a few bars booked rock 'n' roll bands. The average joints presented quieter music; their clienteles preferred good-timey pop, "folk," or background jazz; people liked to talk over their drinks.

Back then, American rock 'n' roll rode the crest of the psychedelic wave. Every city had its small ballroom where, if you were one of the growing number of rock fans, you could see two or three bands, in concert, almost any night of the week. None of those ballrooms are left now, but in those days a new band cut its teeth in an environment that resembled a cross between the concerts of the '90s and a small circus!

The gigantic commercial growth of rock swamped the small ballrooms. It's too bad, because many interesting and unorthodox bands grew to prominence in that period as a direct consequence of that background. Because they were working in concert situations from the start, they learned to present themselves with more imagination and flexibility than the average bar-trained band.

In any case, if you want to work today, you go through the clubs; they are the most important employers of new and developing bands. As you move up, you graduate into more lucrative and less grueling college and concert work. With a sigh of relief, you can leave the cheaper clubs behind. Now you will try to work the larger showcase clubs, as an opening act to nationally prominent bands; you'll do only two sets, and the money will be much better. Don't burn any bridges, however, because if your popularity wanes and your forward momentum stops, inertia will pull you back into those cheap but reliable honky-tonks where you'll be glad you have friends.

Concerts are unusual for a band that does not have an album out, but occasionally you'll have the opportunity to do a show from the concert stage. However, the clubs are where you'll pay your dues, so it makes sense to dwell somewhat on this milieu, and the policies and procedures you'll want to be familiar with when you work in clubs.

CLUBS: WHAT YOU SHOULD KNOW

You have very little importance to a club owner unless you've proved that you're boosting the club's trade. Until then, you are a quantity, a bar expense—like milk for sombreros. So don't expect to be treated as if you were important. This would defy history. For centuries musicians have never been important in themselves—only in their effect: folks love them because of what they do. To their employers they are servants. The average club owner will regard you that way at first.

Deals

Clubs will start by offering a new band a straight fee. Try not to accept any less than your local going rate, per musician, per night. If you do well and are able to raise your fee with confidence, you may want to go for a portion of the door (cover charge) or the bar (usually net revenue from early evening until closing). This kind of arrangement works well if you're drawing significant crowds.

Sometimes the owner will propose a new deal to you, and you will have to examine it carefully before you agree. Will the door add up to at least as much as your present fee? If not, forget it. Or insist on a guarantee—that you get no less than your present fee no matter how meager the door receipts.

Some Common Deals

1. The whole door against a guarantee. If your guarantee is $300 for the night, that's what the club must see that you get, even if no one shows up. If 300 people pay $2 to come in, that's $600 in your pocket.

2. You take 30 to 50 percent of the bar, against a guarantee. If the bar tally adds up to $1,000 (after expenses), you take home $500 (on a 50 percent deal). This arrangement raises a basic question of trust:

Can you trust the club owner? It's easy to misrepresent bar receipts, particularly in a busy club. For this reason I prefer the door—it's easier to watch. If you have any doubts, station your own person there (with a pocket counter) to keep an eye on door receipts.

Sets

Some clubs present four hours of music, some five. The ones that offer five will try to get five forty-minute sets out of you. To most bands, however, five sets of rock 'n' roll music is a crushing psychological load. Most likely you would rather do four of longer length— providing an equal amount of music. But to the club owner, that just means you'll be taking irregular breaks and probably trying to cheat the club out of a few minutes work. Not appearing exactly on the hour, you'll be harder to clock.

If you're a new band, you have little choice but to honor the club's demand. But if you are at all established, negotiate: tell the owner that you do four good shows, which will keep the audience happy—and that you *don't* do five sets. In most cases the owner will grumble but won't insist. In the few cases where you hit a stone wall, you can either give in or pack up and go (if you have the clout to make the gesture mean something). I would advise doing it his way: if you're still at a point where you're quibbling over four versus five sets, chances are you *don't* have the clout to benefit from such a gesture.

Whatever you decide to do (assuming you stay), find out from the club owner exactly what time to wrap up, then stretch your breaks and tailor your sets so that you wind up precisely on schedule. Note that most bar clocks run anywhere from ten to fifteen minutes fast, because it takes that long to clear the last patrons out at closing time. You should have your own watch or clock on stage, synchronized with the bar clock—which is often not visible from the stage.

By the way, unless you're fired, *never* quit early—for any reason. Nothing infuriates club owners more. They need a band on stage to attract walk-in business from the street, if nothing more.

A Standard Four-Set Schedule

7:30–8:00	Set up
8:00–8:40	First set
8:40–9:00	Break
9:00–9:40	Second set

9:40–10:00	Break
10:00–10:40	Third set
10:40–11:00	Break
11:00–11:40	Final set
11:40	Last call
Midnight	Close

The guest list

If the club has a cover charge, you should be allowed to invite a reasonable number of guests. Insist on this privilege gently. Keep the numbers down if the club asks you to. Present your own list to the doorkeeper to avoid errors. If a club owner shows reluctance, point out that your guests are all drinkers and the club stands to lose considerable trade if they go elsewhere. Why should an owner turn away $100 at the bar to save $10 at the door?

Drink policy

Almost every club gives the band a break on drinks; it can range all the way from free draft beer and half-price liquor to a tightwad 10 percent off across the board. Clubs that don't give you a break don't deserve a cent of your money; bring your own bottle. After all, you're an employee—why should you pay customer prices? If you do bring your own, be subtle about it; don't litter the stage with empty half pints.

A Typical, Decent Discount Policy for Bands
Draft beer: half price
Liquor: 25 percent off per shot
Soft drinks: free

Drunks

Bars are where you find these folks, of course. Sometimes they latch onto the musicians. Like children, they're tenacious and very sensitive to rejection. Be polite but firm. Don't let them play with your instruments, don't let them come up and take the mike, and don't stop your show because a drunk is incoherently trying to attract your attention. Tell drunks "no" pleasantly, with a nod and a big grin, but tell them no—and keep moving. If somebody is really making things hard for you, ask the club owner or the bouncer to take care of it.

Bartenders and waitresses

Cordial relations with the club's staff make the night's work a lot easier. Often the club owner or manager isn't around and the head bartender is in charge. Bartenders seem to fall roughly into two categories: (1) friendly, affable people; and (2) haughty, rather
unpleasant snobs. Your best bet is to be pals with the good guys and
humor the less-affable types. Bartenders are well placed to shoot you
inside information. If they want to, for example, they can let you
know that you're being cheated, and by exactly how much.

When you're ordering drinks at the band discount, be sure to
let the bartender know, loud and clear, that you're in the band
(unless you're well known from performing there already). Once
your drink is rung up at the regular price, correcting the error can
be time-consuming, which may irk the bartender. Remember, bartenders are busy people and it can take a while for them to get to
know and recognize you. Use the service bar, if there is one, or the
service area where the waitresses order, unless the waitresses are very
busy. Most bartenders will appreciate it if you don't trouble them for
soft drinks and water, but pour your own—usually from one of those
magic multispouted dispenser wands.

Waitresses in the kind of club where you'll do most of your
work are underpaid and intensely overworked. Though most of
them put their most pleasant face on, they receive a lot of abuse
from customers and are usually in no mood to get any more from
the band. Treat them well; they are the only people in the club lower
on the totem pole than you are. Always remind the crowd to tip
heavily and often—without tips, the waitresses' work night is a waste
of time.

Bouncers and doorkeepers

To make a fan of the bouncer is to shift a subtle but undeniable balance of power in your favor. If you alienate the bouncer, you
deserve whatever you get. Bouncers are usually nice guys, jocks who
like music and are friendly to the band. Occasionally you'll
encounter one with a snotty attitude who is a flunky for the owner
or manager, or is bucking for a promotion, so do your best not to
let it bother you.

Managers and owners

Sometimes the club's manager and owner are one and the same; in
larger clubs, you will most likely be dealing with the manager. It's

best to have as little to do with managers as possible during the evening—except to exchange pleasantries. Most will leave you alone and will expect the same in return. Don't bother them with trifles. Take it up with the bartender. Some bar managers think they are impresarios and will be all over you—demanding that you play this or that, and forever hustling you up on stage ("You're two minutes late! Get up there!"). Some will hardly make an appearance and never say a word to you.

If you do have a beef with the club owner or manager, keep the level of emotional intensity down and make your point with quiet, insistent logic. They often have quick tempers and are tougher than you are.

Good club managers are as attentive to their relations with the band as they are to any other aspect of their operation. They know that a happy band performs better than a disgruntled, hostile band. One of my favorite club managers used to send up a tray of each band member's favorite drinks halfway through the final set. This sort of gesture will always put the band in a mood to finish strong.

Equipment

For some unknown reason, musicians are never consulted when a club owner builds a stage. Most stages are awkwardly shaped, too small for the average band, and disadvantageously placed for acoustics. Setting up is sometimes a multilevel engineering problem, so give yourself time to work it out—don't show up at the last minute. Setting up early in the day is best, especially if you plan to do an elaborate sound check, because only a handful of people will be there (avoid lunch hour, however). If the club is open only in the evening, ask the club owner for a specific pre-opening time for you to unload and set up. The solution may be as simple as arranging for the head bartender to unlock the doors a half-hour early.

During an engagement of several nights, it's a good rule to leave only your heavy equipment set up overnight. Every band has a tale to tell of equipment stolen from a club, so you might as well minimize the hazard. Take your mike, instruments, accessory pedals, and amplifier heads. The drummer should take the cymbals and perhaps the snare. Sometimes the club has a locked room for equipment, which reduces (although not totally) the possibility of theft. The club owner's office itself is usually a pretty fair bet. And if you don't want your amps used on the sly by auditioning bands, take your fuses and fuse caps.

Rip-offs continue during show time, of course, and while you're on stage your spare equipment, coats, and anything else of value should be stashed in a safe place—the checkroom, the club owner's office, under the stage, or behind your amp.

While you're playing, protect your equipment. Drunk or delirious dancers knock over PA columns, pitch headlong into drum sets, and fall into mike stands, sending mikes smashing to the floor or (if you're singing) directly into your teeth. Tell people to keep back. But if the mayhem continues, push them back physically or raise your boot and give them a shove—it works, and it feels terrific!

Getting paid

Get your money every night if possible. This is one way to avoid being underpaid at the end of your engagement. You'll have to wait until the night's receipts have been counted, so relax for a while, but make it clear by your continued presence that you aren't going anywhere until you have the money. If the club pays you by check, ask them to cash it for you immediately; this is common practice when there is cash on hand (following a good night's business). If only three customers showed up, you'll have to take the check to the bank next morning and cash it. Don't deposit it. If the check is bad, you want to know immediately, not a week later.

If for any reason the club owner claims that you can't be paid on the spot, make an arrangement to meet the next day or have the money left with the day bartender. Call before you make a needless trip, to avoid that classic delaying technique of club owners: the no-show. If you have reason to trust the club owner, accept an offer of two nights' pay at the close of business the following night. But if it appears you are in the process of getting stiffed, and the particular club has a reputation for failing to pay, politely demand your *first* night's pay before starting—or at least before completing—your second night's work.

And when you leave the club with all that money, be careful. Don't leave alone if you can help it. There are those who know you're carrying a payroll and would be delighted to relieve you of the burden.

COLLEGES AND SCHOOLS:
NICE WORK IF YOU CAN GET IT

College gigs are a welcome change of pace from the club circuit. Because they generally fall into the category of weekend one-nighters, it's hard to exist on college gigs alone, unless you are a weekend band. They offer formidable advantages: the pay is distinctly better, the work load usually lighter, the audiences are more fun, and the working conditions more comfortable. Never be afraid to double your asking price when negotiating college jobs. Even if you don't get it, that's where you should start. Dealing directly with college kids is usually refreshing—although you'll occasionally encounter a campus "music-biz" type who seems to be preparing to enter that business by imitating the worst examples of it.

CAMPUS PERFORMANCE OPPORTUNITIES

Here are most of the working situations you'll get on the campus, with approximate 1990s pay ranges.

1. Fraternity parties: $200 to $300. Pretty low-down. Watch out for flying beer. The rowdiest situations available.

2. Campus tavern: $250 to $350. Unlike the average club, you're usually through by midnight.

3. Open dance or mixer: $350 to $700. These are held in gyms, campus armories, or other large spaces. They're usually sponsored by an organization, the student council or some other outfit with an entertainment budget.

4. Outdoor special: $450 to $1,000. Beer blasts, celebrations of spring, Fall Weekend—almost any excuse can provide the occasion. It's usually an informal concert situation; you play from a portable stage and most likely share the bill with one or two other bands.

5. Minor concert: $750 to $1,500. This usually links you up as opening act to a local band whose name is beginning to attract a lot of attention. You aren't the biggie yet—and the headliners aren't very big either—but their name is solid enough to draw a small concert crowd, and everyone expects them to break nationally at any time.

6. Opening act for a major concert: $1,000 to $2,000. These will hardly come your way at this point. This sort of work usually goes to the "headliner" described above. If lightning should strike, however, the experience can be breathtaking. It can also form the foundation of a publicity blitz that will help you pick up better work overnight.

7. High-school dance: $250 to $400. Don't forget the high schools. But be on your best behavior. Solicitous parents and teachers are on guard to check rowdiness, and you will get close scrutiny.

At most college gigs, you can expect to be paid in the form of a cashier's check, which you will not be able to cash on the spot. There's nothing you can do about it, because this is the way colleges pay for things. At least you'll know the check is good, so don't worry about cashing it immediately, as you might in the case of a club.

Have fun! Use and enjoy the campus. If you're on the road and have time to kill, campuses are full of diversions. Food and drink are cheaper on campus, and of passable quality. And if you're feeling down and dirty, there are great showers in any dorm.

If you're beginning to get college gigs, this is a sign that you're rising out of the heap. Don't let up. Keep doing your absolute best; word spreads among campuses, and if the grapevine is singing with your name, you'll get lots of work on the college circuit. Believe me: arriving at a $1,000 miniconcert to find a tub of beer and soft drinks, as well as a tray of sandwiches and a fifth of your favorite liquor, is an inherently superior experience to working a club.

CONCERTS VERSUS CLUBS

As you encounter more and more concert-style occasions, you'll observe a fundamental irony: the work is easier and you get more money for it. But in another sense much more is demanded of you: that single show must be right on target. Unlike clubs, where you spread yourself out over an entire evening (and people are often watching each other as much as they're watching you), concerts put you under close scrutiny for a short, intense period of time by thousands of people who will perhaps form a permanent impression of you from that one performance.

Some bands don't perceive or accept this fundamental discrepancy. Their attitude is "We'll just be ourselves up there; we are what we are—why try to be anything more?" But a bar band's approach is often too loose and unpaced to hold a concert audience. So the unintended result is that thousands leave the concert thinking, "What a dud," whereas with some preparation, the same band might have put across a tight, exciting show.

The stakes are definitely higher for you in a concert situation. More is on the line, minute for minute, number for number, so you owe it to yourselves to be prepared. Don't make the mistake of staying on too long when you're opening for the crowd favorite. Use your strongest material, do a short set, and get off, leaving a pleasant, rather than tiresome, impression. As you can imagine, the hours are great for an opening act. You can be home by ten—unheard of

Fundamental Differences between Performing in a Concert vs. a Club

Club	Concert
Lots of material, some of it less than your best.	Only your absolute best stuff. No filler, no padding.
Stamina required to play three to five hours.	Concentration required to play one perfect hour.
Lots of audience contact. They're only a few feet away and you mingle with them on breaks.	Little direct audience contact. The physical distance gives you an element of theatrical control that's harder to maintain in a club where the action is all around you.
There's a demand for dance material.	No pressure for dance material—although it's an effective crowd-pleaser in any context.
Sets can be sloppy and improvisational without sacrificing rapport (not that they ought to be, however!); people are often talking and moving around, and you can get away with murder.	Well-drilled show, carefully paced, is necessary to hold concert crowd's critical respect. Nobody's there to do anything but watch you, so you bear the total responsibility for making things happen.

for a bar band! Once you start doing concerts, you'll never want to do anything else. And if your aim is to go all the way, this is the sort of work you'll end up doing almost exclusively.

At this point, however, you're probably still struggling to get into your local clubs—and that's as it should be, when you recall that most bands have been together at least three to five years before they begin to break through on a significant level. Meanwhile, there's a lot to learn about presenting yourselves to an audience. That's what chapter 7 is about.

7

BASIC SHOWMANSHIP

S howmanship—the way you present the band, visually and verbally—requires you to accept the attitude that what you're doing, on some level, is pure theater. Some musicians have trouble with this: they feel it cheapens them to have to "shake their ass." It's the Miles Davis syndrome: he never catered to his audience, showing his disdain for theatrics by turning his back on them. But Miles Davis was a genius—and anyway, rock 'n' roll isn't just pure music and never has been. It's an entertainment form that combines dynamic images, personality, and body-moving music. This makes it unlike jazz, unlike "folk," and certainly unlike classical music. Rock 'n' roll is musical theater pretending *not* to be theater. It's a show.

The mood of the audience reflects, or resonates with, the mood and energy of the band. If the band is nervous, fumbling, or uncomfortable, the audience will tighten up. The crowd identifies with the band—as long as the band can capture its imagination. But if no energy is coming off the stage, the identification process won't happen. All that remains is distance between band and audience, distance that grows until the audience is just a cold observer, peering at the band through the wrong end of a telescope.

MAKE YOUR IMAGE WORK FOR YOU

First, you must discover your collective image. Then begin to create it—to tinker with it consciously. Don't rush this process, but don't avoid facing it. It's important to have a strong sense of who you are, on stage. This awareness should include an understanding of who your fans are, what their lifestyle is, and what kind of stage imagery appeals to them and supports, rather than mocks, your personality.

Long hair, short hair? Rayon or rawhide? Think hard. Analyze the band's image with as little vanity as possible. And once you have a clear picture of who is standing on that stage, learn to exploit the means for projecting the picture as vividly as possible: what you wear, how you move, what you say.

WHAT YOU WEAR

Dress according to your image. Dress up to it, or down to it, and then don't betray it. If your style of dress clashes with your style of music, it's confusing to an audience. Unless ambiguity is somehow a part of your image, you should try to avoid it. If your music is sweet and introspective, for instance, you shouldn't wear clear plexiglass jumpsuits and spray your skin silver; leave that for the flash bands.

Stage dress should be largely a matter of habit and rule. Otherwise you're always tempted to show up at the gig in your street clothes. You probably haven't struck it rich yet, so buy your stage clothes and don't use them for everyday street wear. That way they'll last. Stage clothes can be a lot gaudier and cheaper than clothes you would normally wear, because you're under harsh stage lights and at a distance from the spectators.

Work on your personal image in context of the band's collective one. Hats can do very strong things to your stage image. If you are bald, for instance, people will assume there is hair under the hat. A hat with a brim will hide your eyes under stage lighting. The effect of this may be to give you a forbidding or mysterious appearance. Is this what you want? It may work against your image. Some people aren't "hat types" to begin with!

One final word: it gets hot on club stages, so light, loose clothing is what you want. If you dress in layers or have to wear something that doesn't breathe, like imitation leather, you'll sweat to death.

WHAT YOU SAY

Some bands are blessed with a good leader who is able to talk to an audience; some aren't. Bad stage talkers can suffer either from (1) overconfidence, leading to a flow of mindless, ego-ridden tripe; or (2) underconfidence, leading to a fumbling, nervous presence. Every band should decide who talks, when, and what they say. You must impose that minimum of control. If you have trouble talking spontaneously, then don't try to improvise; think of what you want to say beforehand, try it out, and if it doesn't work, revise it or scrap it and come up with something new. The worst thing you can do is refuse to face the problem—to go on, night after night, sounding stupid whenever you stop to talk.

When you front a band, there are certain bases you must touch. You must say the name of the band from time to time; you must announce where else the band can be seen in the near future; you must make any announcements the club requests you to make; and you really ought to remind the crowd to tip waitresses and bartenders. This is the minimum—but only the minimum. Your real job is to establish a verbal identity for the band. Once you open your mouth, the audience's perception of your image will undergo a change, based on what you say. If your rap is tasteless, pointlessly hostile, or hard to hear, for example, you will have violated your image and needlessly injured your career. You owe it to yourself to work on this aspect of your presentation.

Here are some things to keep in mind:

1. When you are ready to start your first set, tell the crowd who you are and how long you're going to be at the club, and then immediately start your first number. It can also be effective to start without a word (especially if the crowd knows you). But no long speeches at this point. Don't say anything else until later in the set.

2. Do not announce every number. It gives your set a jerky, predictable rhythm. But always announce your originals. Otherwise who'll know they're original?

3. If there's a house sound system, and you're having trouble hearing yourself (especially your vocals) over the monitors, ask for specific monitor improvements over the PA. Be nice about it no matter how racked your nerves might be; remember, the crowd doesn't really care about your monitor problem—if they can hear you, that's all that matters to them. But they'll really pick up on your frustration if you let it get out of hand. So what if the monitors aren't perfect? Do the best you can and don't be a prima donna.

4. Some of your stage patter will work with a familiar crowd but should be modified for strangers. When you're not sure who your audience is, keep your talk pretty straightforward. I once watched a veteran New York folky lose control of a college audience by subjecting them to a lot of '50s trivia that meant nothing to them. No nostalgia jokes for sixteen-year-olds!

5. Resist the temptation to aim your talk at friends in the club. You should always maintain a slightly formal relationship with your audience. Don't project cliquishness. This goes double for band in-

jokes. Because no one but the band will understand them, you will just appear to be laughing at something stupid rather than funny.

6. Don't extemporize unless you're good at it. Even then, check yourself. Have your rap taped and listen to the playback carefully and critically. The whole band should listen to it together. Are you really as clever and witty as you thought? If so, keep doing it. If not, pull in the reins.

7. Spread some of the fronting around, for variety, unless one of you is the "main attraction" and your show demands keeping all the attention on that person. It renews audience attention and interest to have another voice and personality to focus on.

8. Be careful in your use of scripted bits and snatches of humorous dialogue. Some bands can perform cornball bits and it's funny; with others the result is acute embarrassment. It depends on your stage presence and personality style. If you experiment with this sort of thing (and I don't recommend it), make sure you're getting lots of good criticism and feedback. How are people reacting? How does it come across on tape?

9. Don't answer a heckler over the PA system unless everyone in the house heard what he said. Otherwise you're broadcasting comeback lines out of thin air—but nobody heard the initial remark. So out of nowhere comes your response: "Yeah, so's yours, too!" Excuse me?

STANDARD STAGE PATTER

How's everybody doin'? We're the Nomads and we'll be here until closing time. So make sure your car's legally parked, check your weapons at the door, and don't forget to tip your waitress. We'll take care of the rest.

Everybody having a good time?

Let's hear it for couple number two!

Put your hands together!

We want to take a minute to thank [club manager, concert promoter, sponsoring organization]. Without [him/her/it/them], we wouldn't be here having fun.

If you're having a good time tonight, you might want to catch our act at Billy Bob's this Thursday night.

I'd like to introduce the members of the band . . .

Last call, folks. [Always popular with club owners.] And don't forget: TIP YOUR WAITRESS!

10. Have something to say or do when a string breaks or an amp blows a fuse—even if you have to call a break. It can be embarrassing to find yourself without a thought in your head when everyone is waiting patiently for you to provide a diversion.

11. Watch other bands; learn what they do. Observe them critically and pick up their tricks. Learn the clichés, like the handclapping trick (you can make any audience clap by raising your hands over your head and clapping to the beat in an exaggerated way: it never fails to work). Pick and choose from among these routines and adapt them to your own personality. Learn them all. Develop your own. If you don't play an instrument, learn to do something visually interesting. Learn to dance, if possible. You can get a lot of use out of simple percussion instruments: tambourine, wood block, maracas. Practice a form of movement that will make you a visually interesting figure.

HOW YOU MOVE

The more you move, and the more graceful and interesting your movement, the more powerful your stage image will be, and the stronger your all-around effect. Music makes people want to move; it's a bewildering sight to see the source of the music standing as still as a statue.

Some musicians have a natural sense of movement. Others must overcome inhibition, or just find it hard to play and move at the same time. But stage movement, like everything else that might give you a hard time at first, can be learned and practiced.

Watch other bands and find out what looks good. Work it out yourself in front of a mirror, and then learn to perform the moves without looking at yourself. Learn several basic moves and use them with taste. The moves you choose, like your stage clothes, should support your stage image, not clash with it.

Extreme moves, like the Chuck Berry duckwalk, or the kind of superstud strides, posturings, and leaps that have become heavy-metal cliches, must be used with care. They're perilously close to ridiculous; but at the same time they're fun to do and sometimes exciting to watch. If you leap into the air, however, check the ceiling height beforehand. Many club stages have practically no headroom and you can easily break your neck or find your head stuck through a panel of acoustical ceiling tile!

Don't look bored on stage—even though what seems to be boredom to the audience is often just concentration. This lowers audience response and makes you appear to be indifferent to your own music. Look at the other guys in the band. Try to find something to smile at each other about. Try to project the fact that you're friends and that it's fun to be doing what you're doing. The audience will pick up on it and return the warmth to you, in the form of greater response. If you don't look at anybody or make eye contact with the audience, if you try to contradict the fact that you are a performer, then the audience's relationship to you will be equally cool and detached. You get back what you give.

It's hard to know how you come across from the stage because you can't go out and watch yourself. You can come close to this with videotape, however; undergoing the ordeal of viewing yourself through the merciless eye of the video camera is highly recommended. It's not hard to find someone with video equipment who will tape one of your shows for you. Even if you have to spend a little money on it, it's worth the cost.

As you gain control of your stage presence, you'll learn how to vary what you do to suit the size of your surroundings. You'll learn to tone your act down for a small, relatively quiet club, or to amplify the whole thing for concerts or large rowdy clubs. One thing rock writers have never seemed to grasp about the exaggerated stage behavior of most superstar bands is that it is designed to project some sort of image nearly a quarter of a mile away. And it does. But writers sit in the front rows and miss the whole point.

Performing on Stage: What You Should *Never* Do

- Don't tune up for the evening on stage. It's boring, deflating, and shows you at your worst—pouting, squinting, frowning. Everyone in the band should own a tuning fork, pitch pipe, or electronic tuning device and should tune before going on. If you must tune on stage, use a system. Tune one at a time in a predetermined order. But it's far more effective to walk on stage, plug into your amp, and start playing without delay. Also, avoid those corny old tuning jokes ("Here's a number we learned from an ancient Chinese scroll; it's called 'Tun-ing'. . .").

- Don't scold the audience for not applauding. You can't win them over that way. This usually happens at the start of an evening, if at all. Give them a chance to have a few drinks and get used to you.

- Don't chitchat with another player during a number. You have to shout into each other's ears, and both of you will end up missing notes and dropping the rhythm. Keep talk to absolute essentials.

- Don't make faces at mistakes (even your own). Don't talk about them over the PA. The audience never even notices 90 percent of them anyway! It's amateurish to use the PA for making apologies.

- Don't use the PA for personal messages ("This is for a girl who's here tonight and she knows who she is," etc.).

- Don't make remarks you wouldn't want heard. The PA picks up the stage, so when you mutter "Lookit that jerk in the red pants," he may be onstage pounding your face before you know it.

- Don't noodle on the instruments between numbers. It looks amateurish, plus it threatens to drown out your leader who's trying to talk to the audience.

- Don't try to break up your singer. It's easy to do and a cheap laugh for the band, but it falls under the heading of an in-joke—as well as destroying the number. It just confuses an audience; they don't know what's happening.

- Don't jack up your volume every time you feel your instrument isn't loud enough. Everyone else will do the same, and as you chase each other up to "10," eardrums will start to split. Volume boosts are usually assertions of raw ego anyway, something you want to avoid.

- Don't let everybody who asks come up and "jam with the band." Only allow someone you know to sit in, and make it brief. Every amateur in the club will want to jam with you, but you shouldn't have anyone up there making you look unprofessional; you never know when an agent or club owner may drop in to look you over!

In most instances, the crucial difference between amateur and professional is that professionals have faced up to the question of showmanship and agreed to accept responsibility for it. This is the true entertainer's frame of mind. Without it, you'll only be good when you feel up to it—occasionally—and that won't take you very far.

8

BASIC MUSICIANSHIP

ecause this book is about how to run your band, not how to *be* a musician, this chapter will be brief. Musicianship is far more than just a skill, although it certainly is that, too; it's a set of ideas about how you use that skill; it's taste; it's talent; it's an awareness that makes you feel very strongly that something is exciting, boring, or beautiful. Developing musicianship is an individual matter, and begins with the desire to increase your skill so that you can play the music that is important to you.

This is a journey you have to make largely alone. Teachers and friends can help you along the way; recordings of the performers who inspire you can provide perfect reproductions of all the licks and solos you could ever hope to learn, but your own personality is the rack it all gets hung on. *You*, your energy, taste, and desire, are the ultimate pupil, with yourself as teacher.

Here are some basic musical challenges that any band must rise to, or else its success will be retarded.

What Every Band Must Do

1. Keep a rock-steady beat

2. Start and stop together

3. Stay in tune

4. Maintain proper volume level

5. Plan a good set

6. Invent good leads

Sounds obvious, doesn't it? But even though they may be generally excellent, many bands neglect one or more of these fundamentals. Why sound 75 percent good and 25 percent lousy? These points should be thought about, worked on, and mastered. This is basic (very basic) band musicianship.

KEEPING THE BEAT

A band can have everything else, but if it lets the beat wander, it is losing the ball game. The beat is the single most important element of rock 'n' roll, bar none. Too many bands have a bad sense of time and an underdeveloped awareness of rhythm.

Try this test individually. Set up a metronome (or a drum machine) and play along with it. Do you stay with it beat for beat? Or do you seem to rush ahead slightly? Perhaps you speed up when you're playing quick note runs? Does the metronome seem to be speeding up and slowing down? Metronomes don't lie; that's *you* going off the beat. If you aren't beat-perfect, work with the metronome every day. The entire band should work with one in rehearsal. Get a rehearsal model, complete with strobe, if you can afford it; otherwise, mike a regular metronome and feed it through an amplifier or PA channel.

Check the band as a whole by listening carefully to rehearsal tapes. If the beat wanders and the rhythm is uneven, it will show up clearly on tape. With careful listening you can even determine who is dragging the beat or speeding it up. It's often only one person in the band (one at a time, that is; someone else may be the culprit at another time). The drummer, for instance, may tire and drag; or, subtler than that, may speed up while making a shift from snare and high-hat to snare and ride cymbal. This will be obvious on tape and can be pointed out, you hope without evoking a lot of defensive behavior on anyone's part. The point is to make the band tick like a clock. Sooner or later everyone is going to end up admitting that they're not perfect, so if it's your turn now, take it gracefully and get to work.

The drummer and bass player carry most of the responsibility for keeping the beat, because they exert the most power over it. Maintaining the beat is their job more than it is the job of any other single instrument. But lead instruments can alter the beat, usually by speeding up or dragging during a solo. This will also be obvious from the tape, especially if it is checked against the beat of a metronome.

STARTS AND STOPS

It's been said that you can make any number of mistakes, but if you start together and stop together you'll pass for a good band. This is an overstatement, of course; but you can't help observing the grain of truth in it. Uneven starts and stops are obvious flaws, more obvious than many other mistakes you'll make. Everyone in the room knows you've blown something. There's no place to hide; your face is red.

Count-offs

Clear, strong count-offs will get the band off to a confident start as long as everyone is mentally prepared for the count. Whoever counts off a given number should *always* be the one who counts it off. The count has to lay down the beat, clearly and vividly, so it should be accurate. The way to make it accurate is to set the beat in your head and make sure it's right before you call it off.

The band should make a habit of turning attention to the member who's calling off the next count. Pacing is often held up because one person (or more) is staring out into space. Likewise, you should delay the count if someone clearly isn't ready. The leader, if introducing a song, should make sure the band is ready before calling off a count. It's embarrassing to count off a number and have nothing happen: you look like a fool.

If you have a tricky start, one that's causing you trouble, rehearse it. Like any musical problem, it will eventually yield to analysis and repetition.

Cutoffs

Many rock 'n' roll endings are simply chords that are held until cut off with a smash. Someone should be designated to signal the cutoff. The signal itself should be vivid and showy: a guitar player brings the guitar's neck down with a flourish; the drummer raises the sticks and snaps them down for the smash; the singer jerks a fist in a downward spasm, like pulling on a subway strap. There are many ways to do it, but it must be done, clearly and, if possible, with maximum theatrical effect. All endings should be clean, tight, and rhythmically strong. Rehearse, rehearse, rehearse.

STAY IN TUNE

No matter how good you are, playing out of tune makes you sound like a bunch of amateurs. Tuning, like poor time, is largely an individual problem that *becomes* a band problem. Any musician should know how to tune an instrument, and should be able to hear when it's out of tune—whether it's sharp, flat, or a combination of the two, string by string. If you have trouble hearing these distinctions, you're probably normal; it's a very common perceptual problem and you can sharpen the skill with work.

Your first goal should be to get past the point where you think you're in tune but everybody else says you're not—embarrassing and guaranteed to poison the atmosphere. There are several good tuning methods; pick one and practice it at home. It may sound dumb, but spend a while each day tuning, untuning, and retuning your guitar.

Remember: old strings often sound flat at around the eighth fret and above. Also remember that no matter what tuning method you use, the guitar is never *totally* in tune in *every* chord position. This is due to a combination of guitar design and the physics of music (acoustics).

Once you've tuned up using your system, play a variety of different chords; you might have to make some slight adjustments before they all sound in tune. Before long you'll be able to incorporate these adjustments directly into your tune-up system.

On stage, a tuning adjustment should be made as cleverly as possible. Too many musicians stop playing to tune while the number goes on. This causes more destruction to the music than if they continued to play out of tune. If a string is out of tune, find a way to compensate temporarily, or fix it on the run, but keep playing, whatever you do.

Bass players especially should never stop to tune. When the bottom drops out, everybody hears it, whereas only the sharpest ears in the room will hear an out-of-tune bass note. Bass players should wait until the number is over and then tune.

Never put on new strings just before going on stage. Put them on early in the day, stretch them by hand, like drawing a bow, leave them until later, and stretch them again. You may still have some trouble with them, so watch your tuning closely during the night. It's best to put on new strings on an off day.

VOLUME LEVEL

Volume is a tricky matter: too loud is unmusical, too soft is not assertive enough for rock 'n' roll. The problem is to ride it close enough to stay in bounds. Extreme loudness is the problem more often than extreme softness, and this is frequently the consequence of an extremely loud ego—someone wants to feel powerful, gets drunk, and cranks up the volume to the pain threshold. Loudness is partly in the mind of the beholder, and so long as you're within the acceptable loudness range, try keeping it pulled in rather than blowing the ceiling off.

Most guitar players need to push their amps to a certain volume level before they get the distortion and sustain they like to use. If you find you're reaching excessive levels to get the tone you want, perhaps you should try a smaller amp that is easier to overload, or an accessory that will enable you to get the same kind of tone at a lower level.

You should always stand directly in front of your amp and as far downstage from it as possible. Cramped club stages sometimes make it hard, but try: if you are in front of someone else's amp, you'll hear them, not you; and if you're too close to your own amp, you'll have trouble hearing what's coming out—although angling the amp up slightly or raising it to chest level (*never* ear level, unless you want to injure your ear drums!) will improve audibility.

Start the evening at a moderate volume level. The place is not full yet, the temperature is cool, and because volume is a relative matter anyway, the audience will accept that level as loud. Later, with a wall of dancing bodies between you and the rear of the club, and a hot, dense atmosphere to impede your sound, you'll be glad you still have some room to turn everything up. You should leave your top volume range available for emergency use and stay in the upper-middle level. Besides, regardless of old wives' tales, most listeners don't want their heads blown apart, and they are liable to walk out on you if your sound levels are irritating.

It's up to you to decide whether your primary purpose is to make good music or to make loud music. Check with friends you trust. Is it too loud for them? If so, you'd better start working on it.

MAKE YOUR SETS INTERESTING

You can start with good material and still give a ragged and uneven show because you haven't found the way to group your material into good sets. The set is the structure you present your music in, and to produce a set that works, one that is dynamic and spellbinding from beginning to end, is no easy job.

It takes the same sort of musicianship to devise a good set as it does to write a good song. Good sets open confidently, then proceed purposefully to reach a high point near the middle, come down a bit, while still holding interest, and finally end with high excitement. They must have variety, changes of pace, familiarity, surprises, and lots of energy. It takes time and experimentation to evolve good sets. It's an art.

Don't put numbers together that have exactly the same beat and mood. Just a small variation is all you need, but something has to differentiate two consecutive numbers, or the second one will seem flat and repetitious. A change of key might help, but change of rhythm is usually the answer. Speed up or slow down discernibly.

Regular key changes are necessary to provide variety for the ear. You can't play everything in one key: it will become a kind of drone factor, deadening minds and boring everyone to death. Try not to string together more than three consecutive numbers in any one key (if that many). Change keys often and you'll make the set more attractive to the ear.

Each set should move toward a high point just past midway through. This should be one of your strong dance numbers, or some other number that has proved to be a first-class crowd-pleaser. Opening and closing numbers must have a special energy, but these midway "production numbers" should be longer and more elaborate than your openers or closers. In a country rock band I worked with, we used a melodramatic version of "The Orange Blossom Special," which is a hard-driving instrumental, conducive to heavy production. Blues bands might use their most intricately built "talking blues," building slowly, extending as long as seven or eight minutes, but guaranteed to explode into vocal and instrumental fire before it's all over. To close with numbers like this usually leaves the crowd hanging—the effect has been too large. You want to bring it down a bit, then up again at the close, but with less of a bombshell.

Using the set to engineer crowd response is something that you can learn only through a lot of trial and error. Eventually you hone your critical perception of material down to a fine edge: you can tell almost immediately whether a new piece of material is a natural opener, a possible blockbuster, a good closing number, or an occasional novelty. But for a while you'll have to keep trying things out, moving them around, promoting some numbers, demoting others. One day you'll know you have a near-perfect set. The question is: How long will it last before it begins to go stale on you, as all "perfect" sets do? The answer, however, might be as long as two to three years, or more! So pat yourself on the back, briefly, and start putting together another perfect set. You'll get plenty of use out of that one, too.

SAMPLE CLASSIC-ROCK SET LIST

"Can I Get A Witness" (Marvin Gaye, Rolling Stones): a lesser-known Stones album cut with a terrific dance beat. Or "Middle of the Road" (Pretenders): this is another solid, high-energy, dance opener. (Either of these songs can be extended indefinitely with lead breaks.)

Introduce the band.

"Rock Me on the Water" (Talking Heads): another good dance selection, not quite as up-tempo. It can merge, without pause, into the next number, so that the two stretch out into a minimedley that can last as long as you (or the dancers) want it to.

"Drive My Car" (Beatles)

Time to say a few more words and to slow things down with a ballad.

"Fame and Fortune" (Elvis Presley): features the classic "slow dance" beat, and can be arranged to suit any band with a strong vocalist.

"Hurts So Good" (John Cougar Mellancamp): pick the pace back up with this number's instantly recognizable opening guitar lick. The original cut fades out—which no band can do live, of course—but you can go straight into:

"Proud Mary" (Creedence Clearwater Revival): a dance classic that lends itself to a bravura ending. Hold that final chord . . . keep holding it . . . WHOMP!

End of set.

Thank the folks; invite them to stick around—you'll be back in twenty minutes.

LEADS

Lead breaks, or solos, are absolutely exposed, and they reveal everybody's personal level of musicianship, so it's important that they be competent and professional sounding. If an individual's performance level is low and getting lower, that's his or her business. But if that individual is a member of a band, this problem becomes a band problem. Here are some elements of good solo playing that you might find useful.

Expressiveness

Blistering speed is often the idealized quality in solos. But it means nothing to have fast fingers if what you play isn't expressive of your emotions, your personality, and your love of the music you are playing. Instrumentalists who have developed great speed seem often to lean on it as a crutch. When the music invites something mysterious and revealing, they give you a series of licks so fast and mechanical that they are able to avoid expressiveness altogether—and that's too bad. Try to develop your heart in music, as well as your fingers.

Evenness

Runs must be even. If they are sloppy, the individual notes seem to be staggering around like drunks. When you practice runs, go slowly, with hands and arms relaxed. Use a metronome to check your rhythm. If you get your solo together slowly, you will be able to speed it up without sacrificing the relaxed evenness you developed at low speed.

Relaxation

You can do *anything* better when you are relaxed rather than tense. When you have a lead coming up, take a deep breath. This will invite your body to relax, and you'll get through the solo without rushing, jerking, or dropping notes.

Phrasing

Imagine you are a lawyer addressing the jury. You modulate your voice, hit some words hard and throw others away; you raise your voice to a high fever pitch, then fall away to nothing, only to shout your main point loud and clear—before laughing at the whole thing and raising your eyes and hands ironically. This is phrasing. Some phrases are nice, some are dull, just as some lawyers are interesting when they plead, and others are boring.

It's hard to say what makes your phrasing good when it's good. It has something to do with expanding your whole sound and then softening it at just the right time; with contrasts of roughness and tenderness; with being aware of exactly where the beat is, but working around it gracefully; and with well-chosen combinations of choppy rhythm-type playing and long, sustained expressive notes.

Learn to express your personality through phrasing; here's where you get the chance to say, musically, the things you can't find any other way to say. This is the real reward of being a performing musician—you have a separate voice that speaks *only* through your instrument.

Musicianship is a subject that really goes on forever. With everything else that's involved in running a band, it can get lost in the flood of business, politics, and flash. Bear in mind that if you let your musicianship slip away, it's the beginning of your end as a band. Keep it burning like a campfire, and it will keep you alive and well and making music that you can be proud of.

9

BOOZE AND DOPE

usicians are assumed to be intimately involved with alcohol and drugs, and for good reason, because the entire image-making machinery of rock is geared to project a picture of total, round-the-clock debauchery. Because some musicians help push this image by maintaining highly visible bad habits, you might naturally assume that there is some inevitable cosmic connection between bands and decadent practices—that musicians are libertines because they are musicians.

Actually, there are some very compelling practical reasons why musicians fall into patterns of reliance on alcohol or drugs. Demands on their personality and endurance are often extraordinary—and get mixed up with the average crowd's desire to see the band get wrecked. Rightly or wrongly, these pressures are hard to resist. But not to resist can produce disastrous results. Bands just can't keep things together in a haze of intoxication. Nor is it any accident that so many individual musicians die young—of overdoses, or in car accidents.

This chapter provides an informal summary of some of the drugs most commonly used by musicians—including alcohol, perhaps the most damaging drug habit of all.

UPPERS

For decades uppers of one kind or another have been a secret tool to increase productivity among musicians, athletes, truck drivers, and ambitious careerists of all kinds. Truckers use them to thunder through the night. Business executives, football players, and politicians use them to burn the competition. Musicians use them mainly to feel fresh, alert, and energized in performance situations when they are wiped out, to finish a long night that would otherwise have them in a state of exhaustion, or to make a three-hour drive home at the end of the night. All practical reasons, but here's the problem: for the energy uppers provide they exact a harsh toll. Consider this: uppers encourage you not to eat, thus robbing you of your natural energy fuel (food), setting you up for another situation (exhaustion) that will seem to call for more uppers. A deadly cycle, if you fall into it.

Habitual use of "speed" attacks your digestive system and makes you vulnerable to heart malfunctions. And as anyone who has had to deal with chronic speeders knows, it rots your judgment, makes you super-aggressive, erratic, and untrustworthy.

Cocaine produces extreme confidence, and the quick access to your imagination that goes along with that, so it's often used by stars, who can't afford to be anything but their best in front of 25,000 people. To crash from cocaine is a very depressing experience, however. And to become dependent on it is, once again, to bypass your source of real strength, your unadulterated self, and instead to prop yourself up on very dangerous scaffolding.

Crack cocaine has been so well documented as a societal disaster that it's hardly necessary to go into it here. As for the practical aspects of habitual cocaine use in any form, the more you do, the less capable you will be of simply living through the week, much less running a band. If you want to be coked up all the time, you'll have to devote large amounts of money, time, and effort to it. Mere maintenance will become practically a full-time activity. And you won't have even the freedom—not to mention the stability, clear head, and endurance—to be a musician.

DOWNERS: HEROIN, BARBITURATES, QUAALUDES

I will say flatly that if you are into heroin or barbiturates, don't even try to form a working band. Give up the whole project; it's pointless—this is an undertaking you must be awake for! Uppers at least provide the illusion (or delusion) that you are more fit for action with them than without them. Downers don't do anything but drown the urge to act; they *prevent* action. There is just no point in using them unless you want to be a spectator, passive and unable to participate in anything as intricate and demanding as music.

MARIJUANA AND HASHISH

The stereotypical musician is stoned on pot. With stereotypes, as with most matters, where there's smoke there's fire. The cannabis high makes ordinary music sound unutterably fantastic, and brings on what seems like profound and vivid insight into whatever you happen to be playing or listening to. Many musicians trust this feeling and want to be high when they work. But here's a question: Granted the intense pleasure and excitement of this kind of perception, can you trust it to be accurate and true? Is it real? How many times does something you rave about after one joint sound flat and stupid when you hear it straight? And if *you* played it, maybe it sounded flat and stupid to your listeners when you played it.

In a band there's a consensus of taste that must be shared or the band is doomed to bicker themselves to death. If you're stoned, or the others are and you're not, or everybody is, you really can't depend on everybody's mind to be in the same place at the same time. You can't count on a reasonably solid consensus of taste, because the tendency of the stoned head is to become involved with every sound, while the straight head discriminates, saying: this sound is nice, that sound is uninspired, and so on. When you're stoned, communication begins to fall away and the band's performance suffers. People start perceiving time erratically, for instance, so the beat waffles; or someone gets lost, distracted by a stray thought that gets stuck in a holding pattern and goes round and round and round.

My feeling is that being high on marijuana can help you produce some interesting ideas when you're jamming (have your tape recorder running so you can save those ideas!) but it gets in your way in a working situation. A lot of musicians will disagree with this last statement, but I don't think 90 percent of them are aware of how lame they sound sometimes. To the other 10 percent, hats off—but I bet you don't need the dope half as much as you think you do.

As for the "ill effects" of marijuana, the jury is still out, as they say. As far as I can see, it's relatively benign when compared to alcohol and hard-core drugs. However, the habitual pot smokers I know (1) say they can't remember things as well as they once could, (2) have some trouble keeping the details of everyday life clear and under control, and (3) get awfully nervous and snappy when they're down to seeds and stems.

PSYCHEDELICS

The notion that tripping makes you a better band was mostly a popular media idea, derived from the "flower-child" bands of the '60s.
This era produced an enormous (and unfortunate) amount of
pseudo-hip journalism about the psychedelic life, mostly written by
gin-and-tonic types who had never so much as licked a dot of LSD.
Psychedelics are unpredictable, profoundly so, and are apt to produce experiences that make it simply impossible to get on with the
show. Why unleash the hell-hounds and Shangri-las of the mind
while toiling away at your craft under trying circumstances? My experience is such that I have to ask: What in the name of heaven could
you be thinking of?!

ALCOHOL

Obviously, too much booze can turn a band into a bunch of sods. If
one or two individuals have a drinking problem, it can set the others apart from them and create open hostility on stage, which is
disturbing to watch. Have you ever seen the members of a band
yelling and snarling at one another between numbers? Grim.
Veteran musicians have usually learned to control their drinking
habits; if they hadn't, they wouldn't be veterans. They've seen too
many hard drinkers flame out in long downward arcs of self-
destruction. Booze has destroyed more personalities and broken
up more bands than all the other drugs put together. If you work
in clubs, you have a running confrontation with it, and you should
keep an eye on yourself.

    You begin with a couple of beers, or drinks, to loosen up before
going on stage. You take a beer up with you. Someone buys you a
drink during the break. This goes on all night until you're blasted by
the final set. Somewhere around the middle of the second set your
playing becomes thick and clumsy, and at the break you trip and fall
down as you step off the stage. By the third set, you've jacked your
amplifier volume up to hideous levels and your judgment is gone;
you say and do things on stage that are stupid, incoherent, and
weird. People aren't laughing anymore; they feel uncomfortable.
During the last set, you can hardly stand up, and the next day you
don't remember how it went or how you got home. If this is you, you
are inflicting damage on your band just as surely as if you were to go
around untuning everybody's guitar.

Over the long haul, heavy drinking will do more physical and mental damage to you than any other drug habit but one—barbiturates. Prolonged boozing will assist the deterioration of your liver, kidneys, heart, brain, and God knows what else. So, for your own sake, as well as for the well-being of your band, it's advisable to go extra light on this particular substance.

Being in a band is not like, say, teaching school, where the social environment is such that you would have to keep your habits well out of sight. Bands are highly visible and at the innocent epicenter of all sorts of "scenes" that go on around them. You are apt to receive preferential treatment: dealers enjoy making themselves available to you; friendly bartenders like to shoot you free drinks. Availability and peer pressure are factors that will make it hard for you to steer a moderate course. Unless you never touch anything anyway, you're going to have to work at staying straight just as you work at everything else involving the band. It's as simple as this: if you are not somewhat straight, you can't do business. You'll fail at it.

Availability ultimately makes you responsible for the outcome—*you* are the decisive factor. You have to stand on your own. You can't blame life, because it's your job to take responsibility for that life. It's up to you whether you succeed or fail, live or die. And if you let booze and dope get the better of your attempt to form a band and make a living, you've done it to youself.

10

THE STUDIO

I f your basement tape is starting to make you cringe—even if it's a halfway decent home-studio job—it's probably time to think about making a better one. You should consider a professional studio or studio-quality situation. That first, homemade tape served to let local clubs and schools know you were alive, but by now you've probably noticed (having heard it five hundred times) that the basement sound tends to blur fine distinctions that make your band sound unique. Let's say you're doing well locally, but want to expand your base to include the regional territory. You'll have to sell the band sight unseen, so you'll need a better tape, one that will sound just as smart as the studio tapes sent out by all those other ambitious bands. And, of course, it's going to cost you some money.

It's possible to find bottom-dollar or even free studio time—one of your fans is a junior engineer and can slip you into the studio from 2 A.M. to 6 A.M. You should make the most of these chances when they come. But I'm going to assume you're paying. Every moment in the studio is fraught with meaning when you feel your dollars trickling away, minute by minute. If this is your situation, you'll appreciate a disciplined approach. And when the time comes to fork over your cash, you can avoid shedding tears of misery if you got the most out of those expensive hours.

WHAT KIND OF MATERIAL SHOULD YOU CHOOSE?

You are still trying to get work; that's the point of this tape, as it was with your first one. Clubs and colleges are interested in bands whose general style they can identify in terms of familiar material. So, tempting though it is, don't jump at the chance to record origi-nals—not unless they are realistically the strongest element of your show, what you are known for, and your strongest selling point. Later, when the time is ripe, you'll need a different and highly spe-cial tape as bait for a recording deal (see chapter 17). But for now, unless you're financially secure and have chosen to bypass the local club scene and shoot directly for a major-label deal, you should con-centrate on landing new and better work.

Club owners and agents seldom sit down and listen to these tapes from beginning to end. You're lucky if they give you thirty sec-onds; if it doesn't grab them, they'll never listen to it again. So you'll want to present your three or four strongest numbers (you should know what they are by now). Don't include any long, repetitive num-bers. If one of your winners goes on for eight minutes live, shorten it for the tape. This also goes for long improvisational lead breaks—trim them a bit for the tape.

In general, try to show off your most attractive, most danceable, crowd-pleasing material. This is what nine out of ten club owners are looking for, and anything else will leave them cold.

CHOOSE THE RIGHT STUDIO

Nowadays you can find small, reasonably priced demo studios equipped for multitrack recording. They aren't set up to turn out work equal to the big expensive professional studios, but they can easily make you a fine-sounding demo, and allow you eight, sixteen, even twenty-four tracks of recording flexibility. Unless you can throw down lots of money, it's this sort of place you should be look-ing for now.

For comparison, however, check out all the studios in your local area, taking special note of facilities and prices. Go visiting. Studios are only too happy to give you a guided tour without obligation. Chat with the engineers, get a feeling for each studio; find out who your engineer might be, and ask to hear a sample tape. Take a careful look around: Does the studio have an isolation booth for drums? Electronic drum capability? A vocal booth? Is it well insulated from exterior noises? What kind of reputation does it have? Ask around: Have other bands worked there? Get in touch with them—what kind of experience did they have? Don't go into a recording situation with your eyes closed, or with a vague feeling of dissatisfaction.

If you feel satisfied, go ahead and book your time—you might as well get down to work. To record your three or four numbers, you should book two sessions (as close together as possible) of about four hours each. You may not think you'll need this much time, but book it anyway; you don't want to end up needing "just thirty more minutes" if another band is booked and waiting in the wings. Give yourself the leeway; then, if you don't use the time, you don't pay for it. If you can, find a date that isn't so busy in the studio; you'll get more attention if you're the only session of the day.

Before you end your visit, find out when payment is due and in what form. You should also know whether you'll be charged for setup time. Bands often are shocked to discover that even though the session began an hour late, due to a long leisurely setup, they were being charged for every minute. Another way you can pinch pennies is to rent, rather than buy, your master recording tape, if the studio uses 1-inch or 2-inch recorders. Because buying it can cost over $100 per reel (and you'll most likely use two reels), rental is the sensible alternative. Find out the studio's policy on tape.

Checklist: Preparing to Record

- Choose only your best material—and not too much of it.
- Pick the right studio for your sound, style, and budget
- Rehearse "off-line" with your own tape recorder. Listen carefully to the playback to clean up anything that might take valuable time in the studio.
- Polish your vocals and instrumental leads. Lead singer: don't blow your voice by overrehearsing the night before!
- Check all equipment. Lay in an emergency supply of spare strings, sticks, fuses, and so forth. Guitar players: change strings the day before the session, so they will hold their tuning by session time.
- Be sure to arrive at the session relaxed and prepared—and come early!

THE BAND SHOULD BE PREPARED

Use the home recorder where you rehearse to analyze each of the numbers you intend to cut in the studio. You may be satisfied with the job you're doing on stage, but listen to the playback and you'll hear things you never heard before—and probably a number of ways to improve them. Make sure all the fine points and trouble spots are drilled and polished to perfection. Time is money in the studio, so now is the time to work out the kinks, not later when you'll be paying for the rehearsal time.

Listen to everything carefully: Is the rhythm clear and consistent? Have the lead players practiced their breaks? Are the vocals confident and in tune? I don't have to tell you how tense it's going to be when you have to stop in the middle of your session to *rehearse* (at $100 or $150 per hour?) backup vocals that just aren't right. Save yourself the aggravation: prepare.

Finally, check out all instruments, amplifiers, and accessories for hums, buzzes, pops, or other noises—more time wasters. You sometimes don't notice them on stage, but in the hush of the studio they're larger than life, and will be heard in the quiet parts of your tape. Guitars should have new strings (but change them well ahead of the session so they have time to stretch); and the drummer should replace lifeless drum heads and polish cymbals till they shimmer and sizzle like new.

THE SESSIONS

Be at the studio ahead of schedule. The sooner you can move your equipment in, the less likely it is that setup time will cut into your recording time. Chances are the studio guys are munching donuts and waiting for you to show up, so get right in there, get your gear together, and tune 'em up—to the A-440 of the studio piano or organ. (*Drummer*: set up fast and tune your acoustic drums. It takes longer to mike you and set your levels, so you should work faster than anyone else.) Meanwhile, as each of you completes your personal setup, relax, play softly, do whatever you do to limber up your fingers and put your mind at rest. By this time, the engineer should be placing mikes and testing for levels.

As always, one band member, not everyone at once, should work with the engineer. An engineer is a professional who goes through this every day, so whoever does the talking should not try to order this person around. At the same time, don't assume he or she automatically knows what you want to hear. Make sure you carefully explain the sound you're after—and make sure there's no doubt about getting it, even if what you want is not exactly to the studio's taste. Some engineers, for example, don't like the sound of natural amplifier distortion; they'll tell the guitar players to turn down their amps. If distortion achieved this way is part of your sound, insist on it. It should be part of the engineer's special art to help you sound the way you *want* to sound.

A good engineer will work to understand your concept and help produce it in your style. A really good engineer will even watch the clock for you, but don't count on that; keep an eye on it yourself, and if the band seems to be snagged on a trifle, step in and move it along. Undisturbed momentum will help you finish everything without rushing.

HOW MANY TRACKS?

Multitrack recording techniques make it possible for you to record each instrument and voice on its own separate track—simultaneously or at different times. There are several reasons for doing it this way. By isolating each individual's performance, control over the final sound is increased. Players can correct mistakes that would otherwise flaw the total performance, simply by going back and rerecording their own part. You will also have more room to experiment with different possibilities later when mixing the tracks. To record *directly* in stereo, the mix would have to be done live, and if it turned out badly, the take would have to be done again . . . and again, and again, until everything clicked.

Hourly rates vary according to whether you are using twenty-four, sixteen, eight, four, or two tracks. If the band is prepared to give a tight performance, and all elements are under control, eight tracks, or even four, will keep costs down and allow sufficient control over the finished product.

Regardless of how many tracks you're working with (over two) follow this order of events in making your recording. Lay down your rhythm tracks first. When you have a take you like, add the lead breaks and any special instrumental overdubs (don't go wild with these; you want to sound like a good live band, not a studio extravaganza). Finally, record your voices—lead vocal first, then backups.

Order of Events for Multitrack Recording

1. Rhythm tracks (with vocal "guide track," if necessary)
2. Leads and instrumental overdubs
3. Vocals: lead first, then backups

Proceeding in three clear stages cuts down on confusion and saves you time. You'll notice that this system is the same one suggested in chapter 2 as a rehearsal technique for learning new numbers. I can't think of a better one! If you devote yourselves to mastering these three stages and the problems that come up in each, then you'll have done your homework, for both the studio and the stage.

One more word about tracks: if you're using four, or even eight, there will likely be some doubling up, and the question of who'll be sharing which tracks is an important one. Discuss it with the engineer; it can turn out to be crucial later on.

THE GUIDE TRACK

While the rhythm tracks are being recorded, it's normal procedure for the lead singer to step into the vocal booth, isolated from the rest of the band, and lay down a "guide track" (or "reference vocal"), to be heard only in the band's headphones (and used by the engineer for reference purposes). The lead vocal will be rerecorded later, carefully, but for now the guide track is usually helpful, because the band isn't used to playing through songs without hearing the vocal, and can easily get lost. The booth is used so that the instrument mikes won't pick up the singer's voice (such spillover is called *leakage* and can combine with the final vocal track to produce an echo effect).

If there is no vocal booth, or if the lead singer plays a rhythm instrument, he or she will be out in the studio with everyone else. To avoid leakage, the vocalist should be closely miked and sing as softly as possible. The final lead vocal can be done with the singer alone in the studio. At this point, the guide track serves no purpose and is scratched.

THE CUE MIX

You will all wear headphones while recording; what you hear over them as everyone plays is called the *cue mix.* Your first impression of the cue mix may be that you can't hear yourself very well. That's because on stage you stand in front of your own amp and are used to sounding louder to yourself than any of the other instruments. Even though you're present in the cue mix, you may experience your own part as being "drowned out." Unless you're used to it, you'll be asking the engineer to "turn me up in the phones," when you're already quite loud in everyone else's ears. I've solved this problem by slipping one phone off my ear and leaving the other one on. That way I hear my amp directly with one ear and get at least half the cue mix with the other. Make sure the "off ear" phone remains covered, however, to avoid feedback.

In general, don't feel like a prima donna for insisting on a decent cue mix. The better you hear yourself, the better you'll play. Engineers who are not musicians themselves sometimes don't relate very strongly to this. And one special word about headphones: occasionally the engineer plugs something into something else, causing a gigantic POP, loud enough to really hurt. It usually happens, if at all, early in the game, while the engineer is still working on his setup, so don't be in a hurry to put on the cans. It's worth the wait.

QUIET PLEASE—RECORDING!

Here are some thoughts to keep in mind while sporting in this technological garden of wonders.

Stay relaxed and cool. The tighter you are, the harder it is to concentrate. Don't get into time-wasting arguments or fights. Most differences of opinion can be resolved rationally within minutes with a cool head. Fights are nothing but hot air; they shake everybody up and make it doubly hard to get the work done. Time is money in the studio. You can't afford the luxury.

If you make a mistake during a take, don't groan and stop playing. By doing so you may have ruined an otherwise exciting take. Half the time your mistake won't even be noticed in the final mix. And if you're on your own separate track, you can always do it over, so bite the bullet and keep playing. Never stop a take unless it's clear the whole thing is no good.

Keep your head in the studio. Don't make the mistake of drinking or smoking too much to "loosen up." You'll end up playing badly and losing control of the session. Again, you can't afford the luxury.

When an engineer asks you for a level, you should play exactly what you're going to play on a take: exactly, not approximately. Do everything as loud and as close to (or far away from) the mike as you will when the tape is rolling. (*Singers and acoustic instrumentalists*: don't sneak in on the mike or drift away from it. *Electric instruments*: don't turn your volume controls up or down radically.) Where levels are concerned, don't give the engineer any surprises; you'll end up having to do it over.

During a take *everything* makes noise: creaking chairs, rattling papers, even breathing. Microphones hear it all. These trivial noises can "read" so strongly that they mar an otherwise flawless take. Learn to freeze, or become absolutely silent, while recording.

Most studios have a visual metronome, with a strong light that flashes the beat. If you're having a problem pinning the beat down and keeping it steady, you'd better consider using it. Don't let your pride get in the way; that's another luxury you can't afford in the studio.

No visitors, if you're smart. Even your good friends distract you. Strangers or mere acquaintances can be even more disturbing. They make everyone a bit self-conscious and slow down the thinking process. Anyone you allow in should be somebody you are used to having around when you work. Recording sessions can turn into very expensive parties if you let them.

MIXING IT DOWN

The mix (or mixdown session) can be great fun. Here's where all your tracks are combined into a single, coherent, stereo tape. You have opportunities at this stage to cover up mistakes, to enhance dry vocals and instrumental sounds with equalization and reverb, and to achieve the exact overall balance that you could never hope for in live performance. Because your perceptions must be fresh, give yourself a few days between the recording sessions and the mixdown to let your head clear out.

The first thought that will warm your brain when you hear those tracks booming out of the huge studio monitors is how great everything sounds! Learn to be suspicious of that sensation and to realize that when it's all over your tape will nearly always be heard through small, ordinary speakers. In other words, be doubly critical of everything you hear; be hard-nosed. Don't get carried away by wraparound sound. Avoid euphoria.

Most studios have a set of small, cheap speakers that they use to check a final mix. You may hear plenty of bass on the big speakers, for instance, but does it get lost on the little ones? If so, the mix is not effective. Make sure these little speakers get used. If you don't see them, ask for them. One producer I know even puts the mix on cassette and dashes outside to check it on his very downscale car stereo.

At the start of your session the engineer will run through the first song two or three times to get a feel for what's there and to begin setting levels. What you hear won't be anything like the final mix and isn't intended to be; now is the time for fiddling with the tracks, setting individual levels one at a time, and concentrating on particular clusters of sound—drums and bass, acoustic instruments, lead instruments, and so on. While this process is going on, you should keep a low profile; the engineer is not ready for your directions.

But when the adjustment period is over, now's the time to speak up. Declare what you want to hear—and keep telling the engineer politely, frequently, firmly, until you hear it. You're a full creative partner at this stage, and if you want to hear something you're not hearing, you've got to make it known. Are you not getting the full, dark bass sound you like? Say it; this engineer may prefer a brighter bass and has equalized it accordingly, out of habit.

The mix is the end product of all your labor. If you're not satisfied with it, your dissatisfaction will grow steadily each time you hear your tape. You deserve to know that whatever potential those raw tracks contained was realized in the mix; and that you didn't let your attention to important details waver in this very critical stage, or let the engineer overlook anything you consider important.

MAKING COPIES

Straight copies of an original tape are called *dubs*. The studio will run off your dubs for you at fairly high prices. But they'll do a professional job. If you know of a decent alternative service (a friend with pro stereo equipment and some experience), you can get your dubs done for the cost of the tape. If you choose to go this route, have the studio make you a quarter-track, reel-to-reel dub, and take it to your friend. If he or she has access to professional equipment, ask the studio to make you a 15 ips (inches-per-second) half-track stereo "dubbing master." Play through the master once to be certain it has been properly edited—that pauses, false starts, and chitchat have been cut out.

Have your friend make up some cassettes and some quarter-track reel-to-reel copies—as many of each as you think you'll be needing. Listen to each one as it comes off the line, to be double sure your friend hasn't botched the job.

Copies cost money, plus the time and effort spent to dub them off. When you send one out, or drop one off at an agent's office, try to make it clear that you'd like to have it back. And don't promise them to friends and fans—don't even tie up more than one or two for the band's own personal listening.

Mark everything clearly with the band's name and mailing address, the name of each selection, and anything else you think is important.

Now relax! It's all over—you've got a good professional representation of your band on tape. No more apologies for poor quality. You deserve a rest—go off to the country somewhere and lie in a hammock for a few days!

If you're a band with recording ambitions, the next time you go into the studio it will most likely be to make a serious demo with a record deal in mind. That will be a different experience from the one you've just had. The studio and engineer should be the best you can find for your purposes. You'll be taking more care, using more time, and spending more money.

Sometimes bands that appear to have a future can make deals with a studio. Deferred payment is the simplest: "We'll pay you back when we make it." A bit more complex is a deal where the studio lays claim to a certain percent of your advance money, should you earn a contract. Occasionally an ambitious studio will want you to sign a production agreement with them in exchange for free time; these kinds of commitments, made early in the band's career, are usually best avoided. Local studios seldom have the clout to make big deals for you. Wait for the big fish to come along; beware of little sharks.

In the meantime, you've got a good working tape. Let people in the business know. Decide who's going to get copies. Send them out or deliver them personally, but keep careful count of how many are on hand—don't deplete your supply. Someday you may have to rush a tape into the right hands to land an important gig. If you're out of dubs, you might forfeit the work. The studio will file away your mix in case you need more dubs. You, in turn, should file away your own dubbing master in a cool, safe place, with the end of the tape out to avoid print-through (the annoying ghost echoes that mar an otherwise clear sound).

Checklist: Where to Send Your Tapes

- DJs at area radio stations
- Clubs, colleges, schools where you wish to work
- Booking agents
- Local music writers and/or stringers for music journals
- A&R folks at record companies
- Friends and family (sparingly)

THE STUDIO IS A MIRROR

Every time you go into the studio, the experience adds something to the self-awareness of the band. Everything about the studio situation amplifies and reflects your characteristics. You always learn something: about the collective musical identity of the band, and about each member's individual contribution. The studio gives you a perspective on your sound that you are rarely able to experience in other performance situations. It's no wonder that stars on tour (the ones who can afford it) book blocks of studio time wherever they happen to be—usually not to record anything specific, but to jam, experiment, and generate new material in that lushly creative environment.

As you become a popular local band, new studios or novice engineers with semipro home studios may approach you with enticements to try out their facilities. It's a good idea to take advantage of those offers as often as you can. You get some unpressured time in a studio and they get a band to experiment with and the chance to drop your name to prospective clients: not a bad trade-off.

11

EQUIPMENT

I f you want to know about equipment, make a hobby of it. Learn enough practical electronics to find your way around the inside of a guitar and amplifier, and acquire the tools you need to make simple adjustments and repairs. Learn how to read manufacturers' specification sheets (especially between the lines!), and to compare different makes and models, ignoring advertising claims and endorsements (which are solicited and paid for).

Hang around music stores as often as you can and chat with the customers and salespeople; you can learn a lot that way. Keep up with what's new. Read guitar and keyboard publications for practical and technical information. Send away to the various companies for informational brochures and ask to be placed on their mailing list.

Get your hands on as many different kinds of equipment as you can. Borrow amps and guitars from your friends. Visit music stores and pretend you're shopping around; satisfy your curiosity. Eat and sleep equipment for a while; that's the best way to pick up expertise.

This chapter will take a look at some of the more common problems you'll have with equipment and, without getting too technical, suggest some ways you can eliminate trouble before it catches you on stage. Here's a crash survival kit for preventing and coping with the disasters you can expect to embarrass you at the worst possible moments. And a few words about sound systems.

Inventory of Band Hardware

- Guitars, keyboards, drums, cymbals, etc.

- Instrument amplifiers, extension speaker cabinets

- PA amplifier, mixing board, speaker columns, microphones, cables, clips, mike stands

- Effects pedals, boxes, cables, connectors, etc.
- Spares, tools

INSTANT AMPLIFIER FIRST AID

I almost blush to suggest this, but if your amp makes a strange noise or suddenly goes dead on stage, the first thing you should do is smack it hard, with the heel of your hand. In a surprising number of cases this will temporarily solve your difficulty—or at least get you through to the break.

But what if it doesn't? Don't panic. Before you start plugging into your neighbor's amp, here's a checklist: check your guitar cord. It may have shorted out completely, in which case no signal is reaching your amp. If when you wiggle the cord at either end, the sound belches out of your amp in intermittent blurps, along with popping and crackling noises, the cord is on the way out. Reach for your spare. Also consider the possibility that the cord that connects your amp head (the part with the circuitry) and speaker cabinet (the part where the music comes out) is faulty. If you use a wireless hookup instead of a cord, the picture is more complicated, but the principle of chasing down intermittent bad connections (and the wisdom of carrying spare equipment) remains the same.

Is your amp dead—the power light's off? Check your power plug. It may be faulty or it may have simply slipped (or been kicked) out of the wall.

Amp still dead? You may have blown your power fuse. If so, replace it. If it blows again, something's wrong, probably with the internal circuitry of your amp. Plug into another amp. Don't use the old aluminum-foil trick to bypass the fuse; you'll risk burning up your amp.

Amp still acting strangely? Tube amps are making a comeback these days; if you are using one, you may have a loose tube. Check them all for snugness. A tube may have gone bad. Wait until the break, change all your tubes, and see what that does for you. Changing tubes is like changing the oil in your car; it should be done regularly, whether anything is wrong or not. And when one tube has to be changed, they should all be changed (all the power tubes, at any rate), because one tube failure indicates more are on the way.

The problem might be in your instrument. Internal wiring may have loosened up; connections or switches might be shorting intermittently. Check this by hooking up a different guitar to your cord. If the problem goes away, then hook yours back up; if the problem is back, a smack of the hand to the body of the instrument might mend it temporarily. But a trip to the repair shop is in order.

When trying to determine which element of your system has gone wrong, use the "A-B" method, that is, if you think your guitar cord might have shorted out, test your hypothesis by hooking up a cord that you *know* is good. Trouble clears up immediately? Your hypothesis was correct.

If nothing brings your amp to life or silences the offending belches and blats, you will have to plug into channel 2 of your neighbor's amp (unless you carry a spare amp). This is highly preferable to rushing offstage in the middle of a number to start making desperate phone calls for a replacement. If nothing can be done, it's not a tragedy; go ahead and finish the night two to an amp. Finish the set, at least!

If your PA amp fails, don't forget that you can plug high-impedance mikes directly into instrument amps. This will allow you to limp through the evening with your lead vocal at least, although it'll sound like the vocal is coming from a storage closet in the British Museum.

CARRY SPARES WITH YOU

Thinking of the awful things that can happen underscores the importance of carrying a spare for everything. What good is locating the trouble—a bad cord, say—if you have no spare to replace it with? Going without spares is like driving without a spare tire.

Spares You Should Always Carry

- Guitar cords, microphone cords
- Fuses (tape the spare inside your amp)
- Tubes (especially power tubes—in full sets)
- Batteries for accessories (alkaline)
- Strings, sticks, picks, etc.
- Quarter-inch phone plugs

Optional Spares (if you can afford it)

- Accessories (example: an extra effects pedal)
- Spare amp (all-purpose)

- Speakers
- Spare PA column
- Microphones

With this extra equipment on hand, you'll be able to look disaster straight in the eye. You've increased your control merely by stocking these simple items.

Equipment Handling: A List of Don'ts!

- Don't drop a microphone, not even once!

- Don't place drinks on top of amplifiers, especially PA amps, where the cooling vents provide a direct opening to the electronic innards.

- Don't transport equipment, loose and unpadded, in the back of a truck.

- Don't tape mike cables to the floor. If someone moves a mike stand, the mike will be ripped out of its clip (see "Don't drop a microphone," above).

- Don't lean instruments against walls, or leave them out of their cases; invest in sturdy instrument stands and store your instruments in hard-shell cases.

- Don't leave easily transportable (and stealable) equipment (instruments, mikes, etc.) set up overnight in a club.

MAINTENANCE

Maintain your equipment properly and you'll prevent nine out of ten disasters before they have a chance to occur. Simple maintenance is not a bummer. All it requires is a little care and forethought, a few tools, and some spare parts—plus a few odds and ends.

Most important is to develop a certain attitude toward your equipment: it is to be respected and cared for, because each piece of equipment you use is an extension of yourself. So just as you treat yourself with care, you should have the same consideration for your gear, and it will pay you back with trouble-free, dependable service.

If you sweat on stage, for instance, you will triple the life of your strings by wiping them dry at the end of each set with a piece of cheesecloth. If your heavy equipment travels a lot, you'll cut down on damage by outfitting your amps with padded amp covers.

By handling and packing your mikes with extreme care, you'll avoid damage to these delicate items. Remember: one fumble with a mike can turn your vocal sound from crisp to muffled in a single splat; resting a full glass of beer on the cooling vents of your PA amp is just asking for trouble. These are examples of the sort of proactive thinking that should underlie your relationship with equipment.

A collection of basic tools will enable you to handle adjustments and simple repair jobs with ease.

Suggested Starter Tool Kit

- Screwdrivers (Phillips head and standard)
- Wire cutter
- Nut drivers
- Adjustable wire stripper
- Wrenches
- Electrician's tape
- Adjustable wrench
- Vice-grip
- Cordless soldering iron
- Solder
- Small claw hammer
- Flashlight
- Long-nose pliers
- Tool box

For emergency situations, where you have to do something simple but fast, I recommend the following pocket kit.

Emergency Pocket Kit

- 5-in-1 screwdriver (folds like a pocket knife)
- Self-adjusting nut-driver
- Combination tool (pliers, adjustable wrench, and screwdriver, all in one tool)
- Swiss Army Knife (scissors, Phillips-head screwdriver, can opener, awl, wood saw, tweezers, and toothpick—and blades, of course. A wonderful, reliable pocket tool!)

It's good to have these items lying around in reach while you're on stage—especially if you don't have a roadie. It saves having to root through your tool box just to find something to tighten a loose nut.

AVOID SHORT CIRCUITS

Loose cord connections account for most of the intermittent shorts that plague you on stage, so, for this reason alone, mike and guitar cords should receive a lot of attention. Get the best—or make your own, from the best cord and hardware. Avoid molded plastic ends; they can't be repaired if they short out.

For absolute best results, make your own cords (or have them made) from high-quality, triple-conductor shielded cable. This will improve your sound (more brilliance in the higher frequencies) and you can build as much toughness into the equipment as your own craftsmanship will allow. (Doesn't it feel good to be the master of your own destiny?) To cut down on damage to the soldered connections, make small loops at either end of the cord, just before the joint between cord and plug, and secure the loops with tape. Now the loop, rather than the connection, will absorb the wear and tear when you move and the cord moves with you.

SHOCKS

Zzzap! Hurts, doesn't it? That momentary jolt is extremely unpleasant and can cause you all sorts of mental and bodily problems. The basic rule is: don't touch mikes, other players, their amps, or the strings of their instruments while you are touching *your own* strings or amp. Follow this rule religiously and you'll rarely get shocked. Keep it in mind when another player passes you a pick or asks you to make an adjustment on his or her amp. Make it a part of your general awareness and you'll seldom fry.

Here's another rule: if you get shocked, reverse your amplifier ground switch. If you hear a sudden buzz or hum from your amp, return to your original ground setting and ask the other player to reverse his or her setting. One or the other of these steps should relieve the problem.

At the start of the evening you should check your amp for ground hum. Jack up the volume and listen. Hear a hum? Reverse your switch. Hum get worse? Go back to the original setting and leave well enough alone. Now you'll be less likely to get a shock in the first place.

If you sing, and your mouth often touches the mike, the first thing you should do on stage is test for shocks from the PA. Tap your strings with one hand and your mike (or mike stand) with the other—alternate the taps lightly and unevenly, and your first experience of the shock, if any, will be muted. Reverse your ground, if necessary. (*Note:* Sometimes everyone is getting shocks from the PA, when their own amps are properly set for no hum. In this case, reverse the PA ground, but make sure everyone knows it's being done, because it will change the polarity for *every* mike.)

If you're getting shocks no matter what you do, it could be (1) faulty house wiring (often the club owner's alcoholic grandmother wired the place to save a few bucks) or (2) faulty wiring in your equipment. Don't go to pieces; just don't touch anybody or anything—or if you do, keep your hands off your strings.

When you play outdoors, don't rest your amp directly on the ground; you'll get zapped every time you touch it. Make sure it's sitting on something: a wooden plank, a bench, or a chair. If rain starts to fall, get outa there! A sloppy wet stage is dangerous; don't play on it. Wait until it's merely damp, then find a dry plank or piece of heavy cardboard to stand on.

YOUR SOUND SYSTEM

In its most basic version the sound system (or PA) mikes your voices, amplifies and mixes them, and sends them out through speaker cabinets at a volume loud enough to match and blend with amplified instruments. In more eleborate systems, everything—including drums and instrument amps—is miked and "put through the PA." With this arrangement it becomes possible to balance and mix *all* elements of the band, vocal and instrumental, and to control the total blend a listener will hear from any part of a room.

How elaborate your system should be depends on how massive a sound your band produces and how cavernous the spaces are where you perform. If you play at soft or moderate volume levels, you can get by without a superpowerful PA. If you play mostly clubs of small or average size, there is likewise no need for tremendous power, nor do you have to mike your instruments.

To invest in a complex and expensive sound system before you really need it could also plunge you into maintenance and operational nightmares—especially if you don't have a roadie to run the system. Most new bands get along quite well with mikes, a modest amplifier console (amp head), and a pair of speaker columns, controlling volume, tone, and mix from the stage. This is not ideal, but it represents simplicity, portability, and minimal capital commitment—all good virtues for a band to maintain during its shakedown period.

Some common brands of stage equipment

Choosing equipment for your band is like buying a car that everyone is going to share. Arm yourself with as much information and expertise as you can before you plunk your money down. To get started, here are the names of several manufacturers whose products have proved themselves over the years.

> *PA systems:*
> Peavey (low-end, starter packages)
> JBL (speakers, amps)
> Electrovoice (mikes, speakers, amps, mixers)
> Yamaha (almost everything except heavy-duty amps and speakers)
> Crest (amps)
> Crown (amps)
> Rain (equalizers, processing gear)
> Soundcraft (mixing consoles)
> Studio Master (mixing consoles)
>
> *Stage microphones:*
> Electrovoice
> Shure Crown

The package system

The prominent names in PA systems produce a variety of low-end package systems that range from mediocre to okay. They are more or less roadworthy and designed for portability and ruggedness, and your dealer will usually offer warranty repair. If I don't sound too excited about these systems, it's because the package system is a concept you will have to abandon if you want truly flexible, personalized sound. But as starters, these systems are sufficient, and allow you to get going without bogging you down under the weight of technology too advanced and complex for your operation.

Component systems

If you have an understanding of electronics and a flair for equipment, you may want to put your own system together from individual components. This way, you can start with your favorite power amp, add a mixer-preamp of your own choosing, and build or buy cabinets with any combination of speakers you desire.

Assembling a sound system component by component allows you to match your particular vocal style and address the specific problems your band has in achieving a good balance. For example, a big band, with a soft, textured sound, may need more PA inputs for instrument mikes. Why? So the system can mike, mix, and spread these instruments evenly through the room. To depend on instrument amps alone to achieve a complex mix at moderate levels is leaving it somewhat up to chance—and will often result in harsh volume levels and instrumental distortion. (Of course, those same qualities may be desirable in a smaller band with a harder-edge style.)

No matter which approach you take toward acquiring a sound system, you can make more confident choices if you keep a few principles in mind.

Good microphones

The mikes are the most critical part of your system. If you don't get good sound here, you won't get it anywhere, so choose well. You don't need the best that money can buy—good stage mikes can be had for moderate cost. Stick to the established names and you can't go far wrong. And don't drop them!

Adequate power supply

If your system is underpowered, your vocals will be distorted. A hot, noisy club, full of bodies (which absorb sound) puts your system to a severe test. Voices, unlike instruments, must always be clear and distortion free. Your sound system must have enough reserve power to maintain clarity at high volume levels—the levels the electric instruments will push it to. I would say 100 watts rms is not too strong to start with, and eventually you should be thinking in terms of 300 watts or more.

Monitor system

Being able to hear yourself improves your vocal quality: with good monitors, singers can hear if they're off key, and don't tend to sing as stridently as when they are completely drowned out by the instrument amps to their rear. Voices don't go hoarse so quickly.

A basic monitor system starts with a "line out" from your mixer, which carries the vocal mix through a small amplifier to a few small speakers, usually one in front of each singer, pointed up from floor level. As your sound system becomes more elaborate, a monitor system will be included in the general design. This will add to the complexity of your overall operation. You'll need two sound mixes now: one for the players on stage and one for the house. Your roadie may be too busy to cover the expanding sound chores adequately, so you'll require a second roadie, or even a sound specialist. But the more demanding your gigs become, the more you'll depend on those monitors. Early in your career it might seem that you could get by without them, but once you've tasted the luxury you'll never want to go back.

12

THE ROADIE

No matter how luxurious and appealing the idea is, don't rush into hiring a roadie. The roadie is another mouth to feed, taking another slice of the money pie; as long as you can carry your own equipment around, pack it easily into somebody's van, and set it up without having a nervous breakdown, you should take advantage of the simplicity of this arrangement. You'll never be so carefree again. Later, when your operation picks up complexity, baggage, overhead, and extra personnel, without your roadie and various assistants you'll come to a complete standstill. Besides, good roadies are rarer than good musicians and generally don't work for less than a good weekly wage, unless they're learning the job.

The truth is, you can't really afford a roadie until the day you literally can't afford to be without one. That's the day you realize that to make it through the next week—loadings and unloadings, setups, self-mixed sound, and all—will stretch the band's musical capability and simple endurance too thin for safety. If this describes your situation, and it's not likely to change, then start looking for a roadie.

Good Versus Bad Roadies

The good roadie	*The roadie from hell*
Always punctual and pleasant	Always late and surly
Has no ambition to be a member of the band	Secretly longs to be the lead singer
Pays attention to what the band is doing on stage throughout the performance	Is busy mingling with the crowd and trying to pick up a date

107

The good roadie	*The roadie from hell*
Gets all of the equipment up on stage, ready to go, at least a half-hour before performance	Refuses to carry equipment into the club; can't remember how to set it up
Confirms information ahead of time with club regarding final performance times, etc., as well as checks on accommodations	Waits until the last minute to discover that the club owner has forgotten to book rooms for the band
Wears the band's official T-shirt and cap; dresses informally but nicely	Wears a ripped T-shirt and dirty jeans
Is courteous and polite to the club's staff	Calls the bouncer an ugly name and throws up on a waitress
Quickly and efficiently takes down and loads the equipment after the show is over	Disappears drunk before the evening is over

WHAT TO LOOK FOR

Roadies are such a rare mixture of personal qualities that to find a good one defies the odds. They should be strong enough, physically, to lift and carry your gear. They should understand and be handy with equipment, including instruments, and know how to make simple electronic repairs. They should be personable and know how to deal with all sorts of people pleasantly, without the need to assert their egos.

They should have the sort of mind that can handle small details without letting them slip. They must enjoy sorting, ordering, and devising systems, taking initiative, and assuming responsibility. They must have infinite energy and patience. This is a highly evolved type of human being and you don't run into one every day.

What you must avoid are the pseudo-roadies, who are much more common. These are the hangers-on, who offer to be your roadie because they want to be around the band, but have no qualifications for the job (besides muscles, possibly) and no real interest in it. The same goes for frustrated musicians: they make poor roadies because they really want to be *in* the band; thus the job itself will always be vaguely demeaning.

It's also wise to avoid scenemakers, who want the status of being your roadie so they can hang out at your gigs, impress the locals, drink at the band's discount, and play host to their friends. Scenemakers are terrible roadies because they conceive of the experience as entertainment and self-aggrandizement, and resent being told to work.

An ex-roadie of ours was this type. If there was a problem on stage, he was oblivious to it—he was too busy circulating. Nothing is more frustrating than to have to page your roadie through the PA because your amp has gone dead and she or he hasn't even noticed! The same guy was unsuccessfully trying to pick up two women in a New York club while we stoically hauled our own equipment out into Second Avenue and piled it in the street behind our truck. This is not the kind of person you want to have working for you. With a roadie like this, who needs bad luck?

It should go without saying that alcoholics and heavy drug users make terrible roadies. The only thing worse than a drunk musician is a drunk roadie. You must be profoundly awake to do this work. Indulgence will unstring the mind and body, causing erratic, unstable, and nonfunctional performance. The roadie who depends on drug-induced energy may show terrific efficiency on occasion, but this will be more than offset by unpredictable overall performance, plus the familiar slyness and trickery of the speed freak.

Good roadies can't be absentminded, passive, irresponsible, out of control, or doing it for the wrong reasons. Don't take on this sort of roadie, especially a friend (friends are harder to fire), because having a bad roadie is worse than having no roadie at all.

THE ROADIE'S DUTIES

What follows might seem to be a frightening amount of work. No one ever said being a roadie is easy; however, I should point out that road work is ideally a two-person job. Most likely you can't afford two roadies, so the solution is for someone in the band to double as an assistant roadie—for some extra pay, of course. If no one wants to do this, then a rotating system should be set up whereby one band member is always on hand to help move, set up, and tear down equipment. This will keep your roadie sane and hernia-free, and will also keep you in touch with how things are done should your roadie suddenly quit one day. We'll address the roadie as we outline these responsibilities.

Transporting equipment

The equipment truck should be the roadie's responsibility, unless it's a band member's personal vehicle. Whether it's owned, leased, or rented, you should look after it. It should be parked somewhere near your home so that you have easy access to it.

Lifting and carrying equipment is a large part of a roadie's work; you've got to be in shape for it. Band members may or may not help, but don't depend on it (except for extra-heavy items); they're not paying you so that they can carry their own equipment. When things get rough, just think of the terrific muscles you're developing! Handle equipment with as much care as you can muster; don't throw things around, and don't scrape amps against each other. Pack the truck with care and intelligence, and use padding to keep things from self-destructing as they slide around in the cargo area. Band members should purchase soft covers for their amps; insist on this.

Be early in everything you do. Get the truck loaded early. Hit the road early. Arrive at the club or school early—with time to spare. Because you will be the first representative of the band on the scene, you should call ahead to check on details. By the time the band rolls in, there should be no surprises; you should have confirmed the terms of the contract, if there is one, regarding accommodations, starting time, drink policy, and so on. It's important to stress that all this should be done in the quiet time prior to the gig (another argument for being early). During the show is no time to be pestering the club owner to find an extra two beds for the band.

Your setup time should be ample so that you can work with care. Expect the worst; it often happens. When something fails, you'll appreciate having time to trace the source of the problem. There will be times you must drive through the night and grab your sleep in the back of the truck in order to insure that you arrive with time to spare, so be prepared for these crunch periods.

Setting up

Club stages have seldom been designed for the band's comfort; they are oddly shaped and usually too small. Some of them present you with bizarre limitations, and require time and ingenuity to improvise practical solutions. Be familiar with the individual space problems of each player so the setup won't be cramped.

Know how each player wants his or her amp and accessories set up, including tone settings and ear-level preferences. Be particularly aware of what *not* to do under any circumstances: for example, don't stack your lead guitarist's speakers at ear level, causing intense pain and possible hearing loss at high decibel levels.

Turn all tube amps on "standby" well before the set. Each player should arrive early enough to check the condition of his or her own amp. Drums should be set up early and to exact specifications; make sure you know how much liberty you can take with your drummer's physical space requirements.

Check the stage lighting. Spotlights should not shine directly into the musicians' faces—causing headaches, tension, and ugly facial expressions.

Set mike stands for the approximate height of each singer. Cords should be taped to the floor so the band won't trip over them. However, leave some slack at the mike end so the stand can be moved around and repositioned by the singer. Secure the mikes in their saddles or clips, with tape if necessary; a mike can be ruined by one solid fall to the floor.

Test each mike for level and tone. Take into consideration the vocal properties of the singer who'll use that mike. If male, does he have a deep, booming voice? Then make your test as deep and boomy as possible or your settings will be wrong for him.

Familiarize yourself with the locations of all A.C. outlets so that when you suddenly hear nothing but drums from the stage you'll know exactly where to look for the kicked-out power cord. You should also know where the house fuse box is in case you blow one. Carry spare house fuses of various amperages for such occasions, and turn your amps *off* before replacing the blown fuse. If possible, try to find an alternate circuit to share some of the load. At the very least, turn your amps back on, *one by one*, to minimize the peak power drain and reduce your chances of immediately reblowing the fuse.

The PA amplifier head (or separate mixing panel, if you're using one) should be easily accessible to whoever turns the dials. If that person is your lead singer, place it within easy reach, so he or she won't have to go diving to an awkward part of the stage to make an adjustment. Ideally, you should be doing the mixing. But if you have a high-impedance system, the amp head can't be more than the length of a fifteen-foot mike cord away. So, unfortunately, you'll have to place it at the side of the stage and walk all the way up there to make adjustments. If the band uses a low-impedance system, you can locate the amp and mixing panel as far from the stage as your "snake" can reach. For protection from crowd jostling, set it up on a sturdy table near a wall or post. Attach a small study-light to the table so that the mixing panel is never in darkness.

During the gig

Be on hand always, and always be aware of the stage. When things go wrong, you will be needed immediately. Have a sixth sense for trouble; anticipate it. Stay functionally sober and alert and ready to serve the musicians. While they are on stage, they are deprived of mobility and need you to do things for them. The sooner you realize that your role during this part of the evening is to be a super-servant, the sooner you will be doing what a real roadie does. With absolute strength of character and professional pride, a roadie must perform any reasonable task for a band member without argument. If a band member is abusing your role, discuss it *after* the gig, but never undermine the band's reliance on your steadiness in a performance situation. Your self-esteem must be solid enough that you can submerge your ego while the band is on stage.

Move around occasionally, listening from different parts of the room so that you can make necessary changes in the balance. Sound will undergo changes as temperature and humidity rise and the number of bodies in the room increases. Listen for these changes.

Be open to helpful criticism from the crowd and evaluate it politely and shrewdly. Avoid the roadie's occupational disease: snottiness. You are the band's representative in the audience, the easiest band person to reach; people will be approaching you in all sorts of ways because they can't get to the band. If you are rude to them, they'll associate that experience with the band. At the same time, you must find a way of firmly turning away the flaming drunks who will want to sit down and carry on incoherent conversations with you while you're trying to concentrate on the stage. Don't be afraid to do this; just learn to distinguish between a genuine nuisance and the harmless onlooker who just wants to exchange a few pleasantries.

Have tools in your pocket for quick repairs; you won't have time to go rummaging through your tool box in an emergency. Have spares ready to go. You should be able to produce a new cord (mike cord, guitar cord, or speaker cord) in seconds. Stash them on stage, so the band knows where they are. Carry small spares, like guitar picks (somehow always neglected by guitar players), in your pocket.

Our favorite roadie used to wear a T-shirt with the band's name across the front in large, vivid letters. This identified him with the band in any situation, and often gave him a certain authority and immunity from trouble: if he ran into someone while moving quickly toward the stage in an emergency, that person was much less likely to take the blow personally. A roadie should be visible. You have an official status and it helps matters if everyone who looks at you knows it.

The band is on stage; this makes them totally visible, but (ironically) isolates and protects them from direct involvement with individuals in the crowd. You, on the other hand, are in the midst of the crowd, and all night you will be called on to deal with people in different states of inebriation and, sometimes, insanity. Know when to be nice, and when to be heavy (almost never!). And no matter how justified you feel, never get rough with a customer, verbally or physically; once a roadie has a reputation as "violent," nobody will hire the band—and you're out of a job.

One more thing: some bands expect the roadie to fetch drinks for them during a set. The problem is that band members abuse the practice and start habitually calling for water, Cokes, or beer—from the stage. The roadie has enough to do without this. Band members should bring up their own drinks at the start of the set. Waitresses will usually bring drinks for the band if asked nicely. Tip them well.

After the gig

When it's all over, it's your job to close up shop. Cymbals and mikes must be removed and packed away. Amps must be turned off, and accessory boxes and pedals unplugged and stashed. Anything left lying around that might be stolen—strings, sticks, guitar slides, and capos—should be moved out of direct sight. Personal property left behind by mistake should be collected for safekeeping.

Some bands will want you to collect the pay at the end of the night. If the band is moving on the next day, you will also want to find out what time the club will be unlocked in the morning. Always get the home phone number of the owner or head bartender in case no one shows up to let you in. If you're on the road and have a couple of hundred miles to drive, any delay can seriously cramp your schedule.

If the band will be on the road regularly, you're likely to work the same clubs many times over; so it's handy to keep relevant information in a ring binder for later reference, when the band makes the trip again. Entries should include mileage from home, gas consumption, directions, accommodations, good eating places, names of club personnel, drink policy, and type of crowd response.

General maintenance duties

The way to keep equipment from breaking down is to develop good maintenance habits. Vehicles the band depends on should be serviced regularly, whether anything appears to be wrong or not. No vehicle ever broke down because of too many oil changes, grease jobs, or tune-ups.

Damage to equipment can be cut drastically by finding ways to protect it in transit. Mikes are delicate and should never be allowed to roll free or knock against each other. Have a special case or compartment for your mikes, so that each is held secure in a bed of foam rubber. Amplifiers should have amp covers; they seem costly but they more than pay for themselves by preventing amp injuries and general wear and tear.

Tiny details should become a part of your maintenance routine. For instance: go over your Cannon plug connectors every few weeks to tighten the set screws and secure them with clear nail polish; do the same for your mikes. Be ready to replace your Cannon connectors and phone plugs at regular intervals. And remind the band members of their own maintenance responsibilities: if you notice that your guitar player's volume pedal needs a new potentiometer, make sure it's taken care of—or do it yourself.

You should know the basic condition of every piece of functional hardware in the band. You'll find it helps tremendously if the equipment can be stored at your house; that way you have it at your disposal in off hours and can work on it at your leisure.

PAYING THE ROADIE

By now it should be clear that professional roadies are highly skilled and rare. When they are good, they know it, and work for good pay. Unless you're well established, with a lucrative and dependable gross income, you can't put a good roadie on salary because you can't afford it. What you should be looking for is a young roadie with potential who is willing to work for the band under speculative conditions—just like each of the band members is doing. A young roadie should be willing to grow with the band, sacrificing with it now to share in its increasing good fortune. There are a couple of ways to work that out:

Straight cut. Economically, the roadie is considered a band member, sharing equally in the money, with the same cut as everyone else.

Ten percent. Here the roadie makes 10 percent of the band's net pay, somewhat less than each individual band member. (Note that this is 10 percent of *net*, not gross. The agent takes 10 percent of your gross. Your net is what remains after the agent's commission and other band expenses have been subtracted from the gross.) You may also want to put an upper limit on this figure; that is, 10 percent of weekly net up to a figure totaling $200, say, and not above. This protects you against your roadie getting rich—BUT it strikes me as a rather cheap stunt to pull on such a valuable member of your team.

In general, my advice is: get along on your own as long as you can, but when the time comes to find a roadie, be very, very selective. A bad roadie is about as good for your band as a case of dysentery. Better no roadie at all than an incompetent or problem-ridden pseudo-roadie. But if you have the good fortune to land a winner, you've taken an important step forward in your evolution as a band.

13

MONEY AND THE BAND

I f you work strictly part-time (every other Friday at your local Stag 'n' Brew) you needn't spend too much energy brooding about your financial setup. You split the cash at the end of the night and go home. But if you're a full-time band, playing club dates and one-nighters all over the place, staying in motels, and trucking large amounts of equipment long distances, you'll need a financial structure that you understand and that reduces, rather than increases, the amount of time you have to spend hassling with your money.

Even thirty-year veterans like the Rolling Stones could at one time define themselves as a few guys who split up the cash each night. That wouldn't begin to deal with the reality of the multi-million-dollar business they later became. Your own business probably lies somewhere between those two extremes. Can you pin down your financial identity in a sentence or two? Try it. If you can't do it, you may not have given this factor enough thought.

STAGE ONE: CASH AND CARRY

Most new bands remain in this stage for a while. Money is simply split up among the band members. Expenses are minimal because work is local and there's not that much of it anyway. All equipment is owned by individuals, not by the band in common. But no matter how informal the band's arrangement, someone must handle the money and keep an informal record of what came in and what went out.

Get a four-column account ledger at any stationery store. Use one page per gig. At the top of the page write down the date, the name of the place, and any other pertinent information—like who paid you, relevant phone numbers, and so on. Then enter your *gross pay* (the total amount you received), and subtract your *expenses* (itemize them) to get your *net pay* (what you take home). In a separate spot on the same page make a note of how the money was split up and how much each band member took home.

Bistro Club, August 4, 1995
Paid by Dick

	1		2		3		4	
Gross Pay	500	00						
Expenses								
Gas: Truck	21	00						
Gas: Car	12	00						
Tolls	3	50						
Agency: (10%)	50	00						
Total	88	50						
Net Pay	411	50						
Wages								
Charlie	82	30						
Bill	82	30						
Keith	82	30						
Mick	82	30						
Brian	82	30						

Cash is great, but it's unwieldy. When you know the band will be in business for a while, you should open a checking account, in the band's name, at a convenient local bank. If you have to pay everyone exactly $56.76, to the penny, it's a lot easier to do it by check. It's also more convenient to pay by check for goods and services. Your deposit slips, canceled checks, checkbook ledger, and monthly bank statement constitute a very effective record-keeping system and a convenient way of double-checking your accounting. For these and other reasons, you should consider using the bank as soon as possible, especially if the band begins to settle into the next stage of business growth.

STAGE TWO: EXISTENTIAL PARTNERSHIP

This stage is characterized by long-range confidence in the band. Everyone intends to stick around for the duration. There's a feeling that sacrifices made now will be more than made up for soon enough.

The band's expenses will now begin to include promotional material, a studio tape, heavier road expenses, and capital items, like an equipment truck or a new PA. These costs will be shared collectively. The members of the band consider themselves partners in a developing enterprise. This means the band may be wise to start setting money aside for the future. If work is regular enough, you might want to set a steady salary figure and bank the surplus in fat weeks, so that you can supplement your pay in a lean week. You may even want to start a vacation fund so that when the time comes to take a few weeks off, you'll have some pay to take along.

Banks, of course, don't lend money to "existential" partnerships, so if you anticipate a need for credit—and it will come up, you can be sure—any loan, or credit financing, will have to be set up in the name of an individual. If somebody in the band has a (non-debit) Mastercard or Visa, he or she is probably eligible for a few hundred dollars credit. On principle, I believe everyone should apply for these cards, to use (only rarely) on band business. The fact is, today America trusts you only if you can produce a credit card (try renting a car without one!). So go get one! Just don't fall into their clutches by running up a large personal balance, because then they've got you—at 18 percent interest per year! (Interest rates vary, by the way—shop around: banks based in Arkansas, for example, offer cards with 9 percent annual rates or lower!)

STAGE THREE: INCORPORATION

By the time you incorporate, you'll be beyond the scope of this book. Incorporating the band gives it a legal status of its own. The Band, Inc. can now employ its members. After paying salaries and expenses, it can invest, as a corporation, in other enterprises. Bands have become owners of laundromats, apartment buildings, night-clubs, and restaurants. Like any business, you'll have professional advisors taking care of your affairs, and certainly a manager behind it all. If you've made it this far, my compliments.

CLEAR POLICIES HELP YOU
MAKE CLEAR DECISIONS

Long before the band ever incorporates, however, problems will arise that can't be solved unless you've worked out fair policies for dealing with the members of the band as individuals. Some of these are classic band headaches.

Vehicle depreciation

An individual who uses a personal car or van regularly for band transportation will realize after a while that slowly but surely, the vehicle is being sacrificed to "the band." You should anticipate this with a policy that fairly reimburses whoever is doing the hauling for wear and tear and general maintenance.

The unsung manager

The band member who handles managerial and booking duties is working overtime; a good job here deserves compensation. The band should have a policy that takes this and other extra work done by band members into consideration. Because a manager would take at least 10 percent for his labors, 5 percent is certainly not too much to give your unsung manager over and above the normal split.

The big debt

You've had equipment stolen and you're paying for it by withholding a certain portion of the band's weekly gross pay. A new member joins the band: Is it fair to make the newcomer participate in this sacrifice? After all, this individual wasn't even a band member at the time of the theft. On the other hand, anybody joining "the band" should be prepared to take on its burdens, right? Better have a policy.

Bands have a tendency to evade issues like these; then they pay the price later, in poor morale and confusion. Vague and sloppy business relationships will eventually erupt into bitter personal hassles. But you can avoid all this by developing strong policies early in the game.

SPENDING YOUR MONEY

Spending money wisely is the other half of keeping the band's financial house in order. At the first hint of success, many young bands are off buying expensive trucks and super-elaborate sound systems on credit. Hints of success are merely hints; even firm indications take up to a couple of years to realize in hard income. If your aim is to make a living, you must constantly be keeping your gross receipts up and your overhead down: wise bands travel light on their journey through the music business.

Sometimes it seems as if you *must* have the equipment you want, because not to have it would put the band's future in jeopardy. A band must sound its best, no? True enough, but in the band's first couple of years, modest, well-maintained equipment is all you really should need. Let your status be based on your music and the quality of your show rather than how fancy your PA is, how big your truck, and whether or not you have those distinct (but financially draining) status symbols, a roadie and a manager.

The three stages of band development

A smart band will develop its technology slowly, paying cash in full for improvements at every possible stage. Here's the way a typical band will develop over a period of, say, two years.

Stage 1: everyone carries his or her own equipment. The drummer owns a van. Two or three others own cars. The lead singer owns an old club PA system. That's it.

Stage 2: everyone can now afford bigger and better amps, with extension cabinets. A keyboard player has joined the band, adding a vintage electric piano and organ, in addition to one or two synths. There is alot of new bulk and weight. The band buys a big van and hires a roadie.

Stage 3: the band is generating more sound. The singers can't hear themselves, and the audience can't hear the PA. The band buys a more powerful PA amp, larger cabinets, and a monitor system. All this requires a large, versatile mixing board, low-impedance mikes, and a "snake" connecting all inputs to the mixer (allowing the mixer to be located anywhere in the room). The roadie becomes the sound engineer and rides the mixer all evening. A second roadie is hired. The band leases or buys a truck with a twelve-foot box to carry all this equipment. The van now hauls the musicians.

EXPANDING YOUR OVERHEAD (WITHOUT BANKRUPTING THE BAND)

Obviously this kind of upgrading requires money to be spent. But it doesn't have to be spent all at once; and it shouldn't be spent without a clear and immediate need (not desire, *need*). Here are some things to consider when you are tempted to expand your overhead.

Don't jump from A to C when what you really need is B. Example: don't outfit yourself with a second set of PA cabinets when what you really need is a stronger amp to power the cabinets you already have.

Don't add equipment you won't be able to haul because of space or weight unless you're getting a new truck at the same time. I know it sounds self-evident, but the mistake has been made. A band is a system. If you change one element of it, you risk having to alter the other elements to balance the system.

Before you take the drastic step of buying a late-model truck, consider leasing one. With leasing, responsibility is limited—if the engine blows up, it's their headache, not yours—and as long as you are working steadily (an important factor: don't lease if you don't have a predictable monthly income), the monthly expense becomes part of your fixed overhead, thus offering no surprises. By contrast, a cranky old truck might stick you with irregular but incessant repair bills. And, needless to say, renting a truck every time you need one will drive you crazy (and broke). If you do decide to lease, don't ever walk in and say you're a band—you'll never get the truck. Bands are not well regarded in the business world—especially in the trucking world, because they are known to drive a truck right into the ground.

Avoid going deeply into debt, not only to banks and finance corporations but also to "backers," fans, agents, and managers or producers. It allows them to put clamps on money that you haven't even made yet. This becomes clear when they suddenly want their loan paid back, pronto. Bands have been known to break under the strain of such arrangements. Best to remain independent. Don't let anyone "own" you.

Look for deals. Check on equipment; bands that are breaking up often have exactly what you're looking for and need to sell it fast. Even if it's in great shape, the price is apt to be low; if not, see if you can talk them down. Search your local want ads and buyers' guides each week; unbelievable deals often turn up. Remember, bands are forming and breaking up every week; and whenever the latter happens, some equipment goes on the market. If you have to buy new equipment, try to find a personal connection (a fan) who is, or knows, an authorized dealer. You can often get it at near dealer cost. This goes for sound systems, tires, vehicles, printing, or instruments—anything you might need to spend money on.

Don't add new band members until you can afford them. Do you really need a keyboard player or a horn section? Are you making enough money so that each band member will continue to take home a respectable hunk of pay? Clubs often don't pay eight musicians any more than they pay four musicians: a sobering thought.

PERSONAL BUSINESS: YOUR TAX STATUS

Some musicians don't declare the money they make and don't even file a tax return. They want to remain as invisible as possible and keep all their cash. The way the tax laws exist now, however, you can do very well by declaring your income and itemizing your deductions as a freelance musician—a category that allows you to deduct a multitude of expenses. If you do a thorough job of adding up every possible expense, you can reduce your taxes to practically nothing and avoid the IRS knocking on the door. This is what rich folks and major corporations do. Why not you, too?

Legitimate Deductions as Business Expenses for Musicians

- Stage clothes
- Albums, stereo equipment
- Part of your rent (if you practice at home!). As with the home office deduction, your rehearsal space at home must be used *exclusively* for music making (it can't double as the family room or guest bedroom).
- Music lessons
- Instrument and equipment purchases and repairs
- Strings, sticks, fuses, tubes
- Concert tickets

These are only a few of the many deductible expenses, not to mention allowances for travel expenses when on the road. In general, any expense that has *any* conceivable relationship to the job of making music is deductible. Keep in mind that the IRS views with skepticism individuals who take large deductions, so you will want to keep careful records and be certain that your deductions are truly related to your work as a musician.

Form the habit of keeping receipts for any purchase that might be eligible. I just throw them all into a shoe box, which I empty once a year at tax time. Also keep a dated notebook in which you jot down things like cab fare and small purchases, if you didn't get a receipt. The notebook (or "diary," as the tax people call it) will be sufficient to account for most small expenditures. But make sure you get a receipt for anything over, say, ten dollars.

It also helps to have a personal checking account. Check stubs and canceled checks are a simple way of keeping track of what you've spent. A canceled check is as good as a receipt.

Remember, unless the band is incorporated and your taxes are withheld, you are "self-employed," which means you must file quarterly estimated taxes. Declare your income from the band on Schedule C, then itemize your deductions. And if it's all too confusing, visit one of the many tax-preparation agencies (this is what I do); it's usually worth their fee to get your system set up by a professional.

Money isn't everything, so they tell us, but look out—it's getting there! The closer you watch all things involving money, the better you'll sleep at night. So set up good procedures to avoid chaos; vigilance and routine will carry you along from there.

14

ON THE ROAD

Paradoxically, the more popular you are at home, the more likely you are to hit the road. If you've made your breakthrough locally, the possibility of touring opens up to you. In the most practical sense, "the road" is any job over a couple of hours away from home, even if it doesn't involve an overnight stay. You'll have to have your basic transportation situation set up to handle these short hops. But to really go "on the road," you should prepare to be gone for days or weeks at a time if necessary.

But before you go charging off on a thousand-mile road trip, give it some thought. First, will the gig help build a base for you? In other words, just because someone has a friend who knows a club owner in Key West is no reason to head for Key West if your home base is Omaha, Nebraska! You simply can't afford long hops like that until you're making big money. A $20,000 guarantee for two concerts would more than adequately cover your expenses to Florida, but the club in Key West isn't going to pay you any more than you get in Omaha. Figure it out: in order to break even, you'd have to have a gig every few hundred miles out and back. That is, a minor league cross-country "tour"—and who's going to set that up with an unknown band except an agent working long-distance through other agents (you pay double commissions). Already it's getting too complicated.

The best reason for going on the road is to widen your base, to extend the area within which you can be sure of work. You started off with your home town and the area around it. Now that your local base is secure, your strategy should be to introduce the band into neighboring areas, creating *demand*—a situation in which they want you back. You can't play every night of the week at home. As much as people like you, they eventually stop coming. They've heard everything you do again and again, and they know they can catch you any night of the week. Before this happens, it's time to get out of town for a while and, through your absence, create some new demand at home. What you're striving for is a situation where you can sit down with a calendar and a phone each month and fill that calendar with dates from around your region, two to six hours from home.

The secret of making a road trip work is economy. You must save money everywhere you can. Expenses are nil when you work at home; on the road you pay for everything you eat, everywhere you sleep, and every mile you travel. Your road gigs will pay you about the same amount as you earn at home; if you don't save money, you'll eat up your earnings in expenses.

Even when you do make an effort to keep expenses down, there are other ways to lose money. A band I was in had the chance to go to Canada for two weeks, at $1,600 a week. The offer came through an agent. We were a new band, so we said "sure." Two days before taking off (it was a thousand-mile trip, roughly), we got a call from the agency casually informing us that there had been an error, the money was $1,200 per week—and there was another agent involved, meaning double commissions. But could they still count on us?

Eventually you learn to balk at news like that, but we said, "Sure thing." Our weekly take was now down to $960. Expenses ate into that pitiable figure with gusto. And the final blow came when we realized we would lose some more bucks when we exchanged our Canadian currency. We came home close to flat broke.

The positive side is, of course, experience. Even that crazy Canadian trip had its great moments. Travel is one of the attractions of being a musician, and like the sea, it can get into your blood. Many musicians have no real home. They live on the road; and when they come off the road, they stay wherever they happen to be for a while, then hit the road with another band.

Some bands are correctly called road bands, because they never stop touring. Duke Ellington lived on tour for fifty years with only an occasional vacation. Certain bands are like tramp steamers: no home port, always traveling, never really the success they'd like to be. My advice is to build your band's success on a strong home base and use the road to enlarge that base.

TRUCKING

You can't go on the road if you don't have reliable transportation. Depending on the size and type of band, this could mean anything from an econo-van to a twelve-foot delivery truck plus passenger van or station wagon. From an economic point of view, the fewer vehicles you take to an out-of-town gig the better, because road expenses come out of your pay. There's another reason, too: it's good for a band's morale to travel in the same space—certainly in the early days. Any other arrangement encourages cliques; people gripe behind one another's backs and form factions of two or three. Riding together is one way of encouraging band members to keep in touch with one another.

If the band doesn't own its own wheels, there should be an arrangement with the band members whose vehicles do the hauling, and the details should be spelled out. The deal should cover gas and oil and some provision for maintenance. However, the band should not have to pay all maintenance costs if the owner also uses the van for nonband purposes. Either work out a percentage (the band pays 50 percent of maintenance, say) or a flat mileage charge, intended to cover maintenance costs: fifteen cents a mile, for example. My personal feeling is that the first plan usually works better. For one thing, it actually encourages maintenance to be done, and this is vital; vehicles the band depends on must be serviced regularly.

Major repairs should be dealt with separately, as they come up. If the truck needs a valve job only two weeks after starting to haul the band, the breakdown was clearly on the way. The band should not be stuck with more than a small percentage of the bill.

As soon as possible, the band should think about owning or leasing its own vehicles; then every cost is equally shared. If two vehicles are needed, an equipment truck should come first. Ownership will have to be registered in the name of an individual (unfortunately) unless the band is incorporated; if possible, that person should do most of the driving.

Bands are often captivated by the idea of owning a converted school bus, but unless you are planning an extended countryside tour and have someone on board who can maintain and repair one, live-in school buses can turn into white elephants. For local work they are just a pain in the ass. There is hardly ever a reason to round everyone up in the bus for a five-mile hop. The bus sits on the street or in someone's backyard, hardly used most of the time. If you're spending a week in an interesting place, you shouldn't have to crank up the school bus every time two guys want to take an afternoon drive. And when the day comes that you have a roadie or two, the band members shouldn't have to push off with the equipment twelve hours ahead of time if they don't want to. A passenger vehicle to haul the musicians separately allows you to avoid these problems.

Your equipment truck should be heavy-duty, and sturdy enough to handle not only the equipment you carry now but also any reasonable additions to your setup. You should know how much your equipment weighs, as well as the recommended maximum load for the truck.

Unless you are independently wealthy, you will be buying a used van or truck and looking for a special bargain at that. Bear in mind that the older and more worn out the truck, the more constant will be your problems with it. You can fix up whatever appears to be wrong with it, but it will be back in the shop again and again and again. You may have appeared to save a few thousand bucks on the initial price, but consider its eventual resale value: nil. You might even have to pay to have it dragged off an interstate somewhere.

This sort of thing is up to you. If you don't have the money or the credit, you don't have it. On the other hand, if you're stuck in the middle of nowhere at 3 A.M., having saved a few bucks on the price of your now-useless truck won't console you. Here is one of the rare cases where you can righteously consider going into debt. You *must* be able to truck your equipment on a day-in, day-out basis.

Avoid truck rentals if you can. They are a very expensive temporary solution to your transportation problems, and for the amount of cash you waste on regular rentals, you might as well be throwing that money into finance or lease payments on a new truck.

USE YOUR BEST DRIVERS

Before you start traveling, decide who is best equipped, physically and temperamentally, to do your driving. Don't let bad drivers drive. And don't be afraid to criticize someone's driving. You're protecting your life—and staying alive is worth the risk to someone else's ego. It can be a battle, because often the guy who wants most to drive is the worst possible choice for the job. Because this is a decision involving the safety of your life and property, you have to be realistic and practical—and tough-minded about it.

SOME ROAD TIPS

AAA

Someone in the band should be a member of AAA or a similar auto club in case you need emergency road service. The fee is modest, and when you consider that the association pays all of your towing charges, it's more than worth it.

The route

The driver (at least) should know the exact destination and route before you head out. (Remember: trucks aren't allowed on many urban parkways and scenic highways.) Get a copy of the Rand McNally Road Atlas so that all trips can be planned ahead of time. Here's where your ring binder can furnish road information from former trips.

Mutual support

If you're traveling together in two vehicles, stay within sight of each other if possible; if not, at least take the same route. If the equipment truck breaks down, more can be done if the passenger vehicle is immediately aware of the situation. Look out for each other. Try using a CB radio to relay information from truck to car without even slowing down.

Gas

Gas up before leaving town. Know where the cheapest prices can be found. Don't get stuck on the interstate, needing gas, ten minutes out of town. Carry extra gas, in a fuel can, and several quarts of oil for emergencies.

Leave on time

Don't plan to roll up to the club one minute before show time. Allow yourself an extra hour for an unforeseen traffic jam, a flat tire, or a wrong turn.

FREE-RIDE POLICY

How many friends, kids, wives, or girl or boy friends can you haul to the gig? If you only work occasionally, this doesn't become a problem. But if your travel situation is habitual and regular, there has to be a limit to the number of bodies you travel with, and a policy for determining who goes along.

It's natural to assume that you should be able to bring a friend unannounced, but if everyone does that, five or six people suddenly become ten or twelve, and everyone ends up cramped and uncomfortable. If the trip is an overnighter, the problem is compounded; where will everyone sleep? Single band members end up on the floor so that couples can have the beds. No one has space or privacy. This sort of overcrowding can build into resentment, and with all such situations it's best to head off pressure before it builds up.

There are two ways to live on the road; one is to bring everyone along—your entire entourage, including dogs—and the other is to restrict the traveling core to the band, period, with occasional special exceptions.

Unless you're a rich band, and even then, the first solution is a sure road to chaos and bankruptcy. On the other hand, your personal feelings about the relationships involved and the kind of life experience you want to have on the road may supersede the considerations of efficiency and economy. If you feel that way, then plan for the number of people you will allow to travel and draw the line there. Saving money where you can is crucial on the road, so let your economy begin somewhere, even if your plans must include a dozen people.

The second solution is preferred, in my opinion. The band is not responsible for transporting or accommodating any extra people. If someone in the band wants to bring a spouse or friend along, the answer is simply to make separate arrangements, meaning a personal car and individual motel reservations. Exceptions can be made on a case-by-case basis. The advantages of this policy are clear: the band maintains low costs and fair living conditions for everyone while on the road.

GOING ALONE

Some band members might prefer to travel independently. One of the most pleasant ways to go on the road is in your own camper, at your own expense, with whomever you want. You are completely on your own, and it's your own responsibility to arrive at each location on time. Policy again is the key word: if the band is an economic unit, but some members want to function independently at their own expense, you must work out the details up front or as soon as the situation arises. Make a policy you can live with and stick to it.

ACCOMMODATIONS

When you're lining up overnight work out of town, always ask whether accommodations are included in the package. If they aren't, you'll be paying for them, so subtract your motel bill from your gross pay for a better picture of your true net. Here are some things to think about in either case.

Accommodations included

Club owners who book out-of-town bands usually have rooms upstairs or a house nearby to accommodate them. Often your quarters will be roomy and comfortable, with cooking facilities. Most clubs make the assumption that there will be four of five in the band. I found that out the hard way, traveling with a seven-man band (plus roadie). There were never enough beds, unless it was stressed beforehand to the agent and included in the contract. I was particularly touchy about this because I like to sleep. If your band is large, be pushy about specifying accommodations for all of your members. Don't assume the agency will take care of it spontaneously; chances are they won't.

Another thing: club accommodations are often shy on bedding—not enough blankets to go around, or sometimes nothing but a bare mattress. The best solution is to carry a sleeping bag just in case; there are many, many situations on the road where you'll be glad you have it along.

Accommodations not included

This means you're going to have to find a motel or hotel, and you'll be paying for your rooms, a factor you should weigh when deciding whether to take the gig. The club can usually advise you. Often there might be a discount arrangement between the club and a nearby motel. In any case, plan to arrive in the area early enough to shop around. The "nicer" a motel is, the more you will pay. Try to find something humble, honest, and cheap. Ask for a "suite." Most motels have them for large families; if you can fit the band into a suite, instead of three doubles, you've saved enough money to cover your meals for a day. Do I sound cheap? I am. On the road, until you can afford otherwise, you have to think in terms of pennies; otherwise traveling will break you.

FOOD

There's not much to be said for American restaurant food. Most of it is badly prepared and overpriced. If you are in a tourist area, stay out of the tourist places. Ask a townie where the locals eat; invariably that's where you'll get the best food at the lowest prices. And there's always franchise fast food—a generally reliable bottom line.

Vegetarians are out of luck in the culture of the American greasy spoon. Salads are awful and main courses are ordinarily meat. If you can eat fish, eggs, and dairy products you are in better shape. Otherwise, you're going to have to bring your own food from home and supplement it as chance permits on the road. It's important to eat well when you do eat because you can't be a hundred percent sure when or where you'll get your next nourishing meal.

If your accommodations have cooking facilities, this will save you money and permit you to eat what you want, prepared by your own hands. Even without a kitchen, if you are careful about it you can cook in your room on a portable hotplate; just stash it in the truck when you're through so the motel people won't come across it. There are other styles of portable cooking if the hotplate doesn't appeal to you: electric fry pans, toaster ovens, and minimicrowaves, for example.

Two or three coolers, or ice chests, should be standard road gear; milk, cheese, vegetables, and other perishables can be kept fresh as long as you replace the ice every few days—and you can find ice at any convenience store. Use ingenuity: salad buffs, for instance, can put together a salad road kit made up of chopping board, kitchen knife, wooden salad bowl, grater, peeler, premixed dressing, premixed herbs, and so on. Be sure you have a box or case for the utensils; otherwise they'll be lost for sure within a day or two.

The most important thing about food is to *eat*, no matter what style you choose; eat regularly and eat well. Don't try to exist on the road on a diet of soft drinks, pizza, and candy bars.

MONEY

The band should not leave home without enough ready cash to cover normal expenses—including perhaps a pay-in-advance motel policy. Individuals should have some money in their pockets as well. Some bands provide each member a daily allowance while on the road, some just negotiate cash advances on an individual basis. Remember that you might not see the cash from your first gig for a couple of days, so set yourself up accordingly.

If you're on the road for an extended period, don't carry the accumulating cash around for long; you're asking for trouble. Hold out what you'll need for advances and expenses and have the rest converted into a cashier's check, which can be done at any bank. Then simply mail the check home to your bank with a deposit slip, and you've outwitted temptation and misfortune.

BAND FATIGUE

Too much time on the road, or too many nights of unrelieved work, can wear you down. Though now it may seem as if you'll never get enough work, the day will come when you'll be in danger of overworking the band. The symptoms of overwork may not be anything so obvious as physical exhaustion; a burnout will strike first at your nerves, your psyche, and your morale.

Classic Symptoms of Road Fatigue

1. Playing gets sloppy. Night after night of being too mentally tired causes mistakes; and lazy habits begin to reinforce those mistakes and make them part of your permanent playing technique.

2. Stage presence degenerates, becoming bored and cynical. Your view of the whole enterprise loses its freshness and sense of fun. You stop generating these qualities from the stage.

3. Drinking and use of drugs increase. You try to find shortcuts to resharpen your imagination and reenergize your personality.

4. Lack of zest for responsibilities leads to oversights and blunders—someone forgets to confirm a gig, to reserve a truck. Efficiency slips and you suffer for it.

5. Everyone's emotional stability is down. Spats and fights increase. You are less capable of dealing with petty irritations, and other people's quirks get on your nerves.

6. Morale drops. People's bitching begins to have a terminal sound. You find yourself talking and thinking about leaving the band.

This sounds awfully dismal, but the reason I'm dragging out the details is so you will recognize band fatigue when it happens. What feels like existential paralysis and life crisis of the highest order is often just a signal that you need two weeks off.

If you work hard and steadily, plan for vacations. Take a couple of weeks off two or three times a year. Take a month if you need it. Renewing your spirit regularly must be a part of your total plan. And don't use the time off to rehearse! Go away—forget about the band for a while. Disappear.

Bands go on the road because it's fun and that's where the work is. But be careful. You're jammed into a smaller physical and mental space when you travel; everything intensifies, and the longer you're out, the more intense it gets. So eat good food, get your sleep, practice your chops, and cut down on bad habits. *Bon voyage!*

15

CHANGING AND REBUILDING

ithin the first year or two, your band, just like any growing thing, will go through all sorts of changes—some of them natural and slow, others drastic and unexpected. Personnel changes are disturbing but very common in the early history of any band, so no one should be shocked, paralyzed, or personally insulted when the day comes that a band member quits or has to be asked to leave.

LETTING GO

The responsibility for firing someone carries a lot of guilt with it. Poor musicians or problem personalities hold back the band's progress and affect the lives of all members of the band. The leader ultimately has to be able to sense the importance of letting someone go. A strong leader must be unilaterally responsible for cleaning house. If the band functions more like several near-equal partners, the leader is still responsible for putting the push behind dealing with the problem. A leaderless band is not good at facing this kind of action; no one wants to be the heavy, so bad personnel problems go on much longer than they should.

Firing

Once the decision is final, carry it out quickly and with compassion. Talk constructively about the real reasons why you're letting the person go, even if the truth hurts. Don't let the situation drag on; it's not fair to anyone—least of all the band. Treat the person with respect and some concern for personal pride; but don't back down.

Give some notice: at least two weeks, or the equivalent in pay if you have an immediate replacement. Get a temporary fill-in if necessary, so you won't blunder into the position of needing the player to stay two or three weeks more—after termination!

Being fired

Now let's turn the whole thing around. If you're the one who's being fired, try to be as positive as you can about it. You can go through life blaming everyone else for things like this, but to do so makes you a weak person. Your destiny is in your own hands, and if you drop it every now and then (or have it knocked away), it's no cause for misery and alarm; just pick it up again and continue, the wiser for every such experience.

Go out and woodshed, take some lessons, practice, and hook up with some other musicians. Don't slide into the luxury of discouragement or self-pity. And above all, don't harbor a grudge against your ex-partners. They did what they thought was necessary and maybe, in the long run, they did you a favor.

Quitting

If you are leaving of your own accord, you owe the band the same consideration it owes you. Talk to the leader and give your real reasons for going. Keep the door open; you may want to change your mind. When you've made up your mind, give the band notice. They'll need time to find a replacement. However, don't be wishy-washy about the date you want to leave; the band may be lazy about replacing you if they think you'll fill in indefinitely. Give your notice and stick to it.

HIRING A NEW BAND MEMBER

Hiring someone new should be an occasion to improve the band. Don't panic and accept a substandard replacement player just because there seem to be no immediate prospects. Keep looking, even if you have to hire a temporary replacement (make sure everyone understands it's temporary).

You should have a clear idea by now of what kind of musician you need to play your style of music. Players whose style isn't really right for you will often be eager to join the band anyway because you're working steadily. You can and should be highly selective; otherwise you'll be going through the whole thing again within months. Always try to improve on the person who left.

Hiring someone you already know is your safest bet: someone whose work you respect and whose personality is a good match for the band. If this isn't possible, then look around and ask other musicians you know. Who's available, who's not happy with their current band? And let it be known that you are looking. If personal contacts don't succeed in turning up somebody, make up a concise description of what you're looking for and advertise. Bulletin boards in music stores, student centers, and music schools are good places to hang a handwritten ad; some "alternate" newspapers, or local music-scene tabloids, have classified columns for musicians, and many cities have a local musicians' listing service or switchboard. You should take a good look at these ads yourselves—sometimes you'll find just what you're looking for.

Once the phone calls start coming in, you'll begin to realize that many of the people who call are not advanced enough (or compatible enough) to work with you. If you can sniff this out ahead of time, you'll save time and energy by not letting it go any further than the phone call. Don't invite everyone to audition; only those who strike you as distinct possibilities. Even then, before you set up a formal audition invite them to sit in with you on a couple of numbers when you're working. This will give both parties a chance to eyeball each other before making the commitment to an audition.

Auditions

Unless you're lucky, the audition process is going to eat up a full week of your time, so clear the boards. You'll need a place where you can be relaxed and loose; the place where you rehearse is probably the best atmosphere for an audition. Schedule each musician for about a half-hour; that's enough time to decide whether things are happening or not. Don't schedule more than a few auditions each day, or your head will swim with confusion and eventually you won't be able to recall one player from the other.

The idea is to see what the prospect can do. Pick out a selection of numbers in your style; if the prospective band member doesn't know them, go over the changes. Try to find something he or she knows that everyone can jam on. In most cases it won't take long to come to a basic decision. If the player can't handle it, say thanks and adios; if you're interested, arrange a callback for a final audition. Call back your best two or three prospects. But before you close off your list, talk to them and be sure they're still enthusiastic about the band; it could turn out that someone you want isn't interested in you. Life is like that.

Anyone who's serious about joining the band will want to know how much money you are making. Don't fudge a sham figure if your gross pay has been low lately. To misrepresent your situation in any way is unfair and will double back on you as soon as the truth surfaces. At the same time, you should insist on candor from the player you're interested in. If you've had your "callback" auditions and made your choice, get a solid commitment; if you sense something tentative in the acceptance, explore it. If there are any questions or doubts on either side, it's sometimes wise to agree to a mutual trial period of specific duration—a month or two—after which either the band or the new band member can have a change of mind.

DEJA VU ALL OVER AGAIN

Breaking in a new band member will require a period of intense rehearsal. This is a good time to take a fresh look at old material. You have to go over it anyway, so you might as well explore new possibilities, either those suggested by having a new musician in the mix (who may bring some good material from previous gigs) or simply whatever new ideas come to mind.

Working new members into the band will mean a more intense rehearsal grind than you normally have to face. To make this round of rehearsals run smoothly, agree beforehand to make them efficient work periods. By now you should have a rehearsal routine that is second nature. Here is a checklist of ideal rehearsal characteristics which you should compare against your own habits.

Rehearsing with a new band member: a checklist

1. Rehearsals are a good illustration of why a band needs at least a nominal leader: someone has to "run" a rehearsal. Otherwise a lot of time is wasted while everyone stands around waiting for a leader to emerge. Rehearsals shouldn't be run like Quaker meetings. Pass the leadership around if you want; a different band member can direct the rehearsal each time. This is not the ideal solution, in my opinion, but better than sullen anarchy.

2. Don't fear the systematic approach. Organize your rehearsals. Decide beforehand what to work on and make sure everyone knows what's coming up.

3. Try to set up a rehearsal studio with "rehearsal" equipment: small, cheap amps that don't have to be moved in and out of the place. Your actual working equipment can remain wherever you store it when you're not working.

4. When learning a number from a record, try not to waste rehearsal time listening to it for the first time. If you know it's coming up, familiarize yourself with it on your own time.

5. Sometimes it's not necessary to rehearse an entire number. Isolate the spots that are giving you trouble and drill them, over and over until the problems give way. Spot rehearsals can save you lots of time.

6. Rethink old numbers. Some of them can be rearranged and given new life. Others are bummers and should be dropped out of your repertoire. Remember: yesterday's bummer can be today's fresh finds! Give them another look; a new approach could make all the difference.

7. Keep a "master book," a notebook with a page for every song in your repertoire. The master book should contain chord changes, lyrics, notes on the arrangement, and metronome numbers. Whenever a question arises about a number, it's useful to have this sort of information on hand.

8. Listen to your live performance tapes as often as possible. This should be done with everyone present. The tape will tell you what needs work. It will also tell you if you've begun to play everything too fast. Over time, working bands tend to play things faster and faster without being aware of it. Take a metronome reading on the live tape and compare that with the original metronome indication in the master book.

9. Sometimes a lot can be accomplished in "section" rehearsals, meaning simply that the rhythm section—or the lead players—get together independently to work on their own problems (poor rhythm?) or their particular part of the arrangement (double guitar lead?).

10. Get together sometimes just to play albums for each other and talk about future material. This is pure fun, no work at all. Enjoy it.

11. Hold some unstructured jam sessions occasionally; jams unlock all sorts of musical ideas that would have no other occasion to surface. Record your jams for later reference. ("What was that lick you played?")

12. When arranging a new number, try especially hard to create an interesting intro and ending. The beginning of a song has to "hook" the audience's attention, and the ending is what will create

the final effect of the number. You can put your stamp on any piece material by special attention to originality in these places.

13. When you are set up for the week in a club, take advantage of it by getting in some rehearsal time when it's empty: early in the day, just after the club opens its doors. Don't, however, rehearse in a club that's busy: the patrons will go crazy listening to you going over and over some small section of the same song.

14. On the road, rehearse whenever you need it. You'll have to grab your rehearsal time when and where you can. It can be easier to complete some concentrated practice when you're free of the distractions of home.

15. Keep a chalkboard where you rehearse. It has a million uses. Chalk up the chord changes in a new number, for example, or today's rehearsal order—or tomorrow's. It's just another tool to save the band's time by speeding up communication.

16
MANAGERS AND MANAGEMENT

This chapter might sound like a contradiction in terms: if you're actually "running your rock band" you are already doing most of the things a manager does for a regional or local group. Why then would you want a manager? For better or for worse, here's why.

A band surrenders its business to a manager when it becomes convinced the manager will open doors the band is incapable of opening on its own. Sometimes the band has no member who will step up and handle business matters; the manager says, "I'll do that for you." A manager is most useful if your intention is to land a recording contract, and he or she can help you get it. Going after a record deal is a full-time job that requires travel, phone calls, appointments, follow-throughs, availability, and constant presence of mind. In fact, you've probably found that just what you do now—local booking, promotion, dealing with agents, bookkeeping, bill paying, road management, and so on—is a full load and one you wouldn't mind throwing over to a full-time manager. Well, that's how managers—good and bad—thrive.

If you've had somebody close to you handling things from the start, and that person is a friend, capable, loyal, and awake, you are fortunate; this is rare good luck. But if you've done the work yourself and you're beginning to feel the strain, consider this. Your band is a business, and to the extent that you've done your job well, it is a well-run business. You provide a service, and you have assets, a name that draws a crowd, experience, and good will; you have a structure of working relationships with club owners, agents, media people, and retail merchants. All this didn't grow up overnight. It is worth something. Managers will often try to make you feel that they're doing you a great favor. Not so! When you turn your responsibilities over to a manager, you are putting the business that you've so carefully built

141

up into another's hands, on an assurance that this person will care for it with at least as much vigilance and trust as you have. In return, he or she gets a very healthy cut of your income. It's an arrangement for mutual benefit. Nobody's doing anybody any favors.

WHAT A MANAGER CAN DO FOR YOU

When you've found a good manager, what can you expect? The big advantage is that someone is minding the store; you are free now to concentrate on your prime responsibility: the music. Meanwhile, your manager will be providing you with various services, falling roughly into the following categories.

Representation

People in the music business are not very comfortable talking business directly with musicians. They are business oriented and they feel more secure talking with other business types. Musicians, in their view, don't really understand business matters; agents, promoters, and record people in particular feel this way. After all, they reason, the band, the "act," is a product, and their business is to move that product, not to waste a lot of time holding its hand. Would a grocer talk to a dozen eggs about getting themselves stocked? No! He or she talks to a wholesaler. Similarly, an agency prefers to talk to a manager.

A good manager relieves you of the burden of talking business to anyone, representing you in these energy-consuming battles of wit, nerve, and will. Your effectiveness in business is sharpened by his or her particular abilities. Contact between "management" and the people you deal with builds up your general credibility. This is the ideal, the way it's supposed to be. Your manager enhances your operation and accelerates your success by providing you the service of representation.

Contacts

A good manager knows how to make contacts for you. Managers who have been in the business for a while should already have many contacts that they can turn to your advantage. The exclusive agency who had nothing for you before turns up work for you now that their old friend, your new manager, is doing the talking. A manager should have an instinct for pursuing useful contacts, and should know how to maintain them, renew them, and turn them into tangible gains for you.

Advice and guidance

Your manager should be able to advise you confidently on all aspects of your operation, based on personal experience, as well as a total familiarity with your business. This last item is crucial. Your manager must learn your business fast—soak it up and know it better than you do. Beware the busy manager who puts off learning your particular operation. As for advice, it's only valuable when seasoned with sound judgment, and that means a lot of previous cases to draw on. Examine any prospective manager's past; does it check out? Bad advice at a crucial stage of your development can swamp you.

Management services

These include absolute basics like bookkeeping, bill paying, and paying the band members, as well as tax and legal services, should they be necessary. Your manager must be adept at handling money and affairs of business, otherwise he or she is of no use to you. Booking also falls into this category. Filling your calendar is now the "front office"s' job. You or your roadie should be informed of every detail of every gig—especially those on the road. If details are ignored or sloppily negotiated, your manager is not doing the job.

Partnership

I use this word loosely because your manager is not your partner in the strict business sense of the term. However, a good manager is in a position to provide you with many of the traditional advantages of partnership. Managers can be places you can't be and do things you can't do. They can back you up for credit and use their good name to open doors for you. If you have an emergency—equipment theft, for example—your manager can bail you out with a loan. Partnerships are reciprocal, of course, and the more successful you become, the more your manager will benefit as a direct result of your success. What's good for you is good for your manager and vice versa.

Lightning-rod protection

Anyone who has ever tried to lead a band is familiar with the "hatred phenomenon." When things go well, you're golden, but the moment you begin to make mistakes, or the band encounters a run of bad luck, you become a lightning rod for everyone else's dissatisfaction; you're the number-one target for hostility, and the rest of the band will direct it right at you. If it continues and deepens, it can ruin otherwise decent working relationships. Worst of all, it can be seen on stage; it freezes up the show.

It's a manager's duty to take on the role of lightning rod, drawing all negativity to his or her own head, and releasing the band from this emotional quandary. A good manager will understand the psychology of this situation and know how to deal positively with it.

MAKING A DEAL

If you like the sound of all this, and you have a likely candidate for a manager, there are a number of things you should understand, consider, or beware of before you start signing papers.

1. Your manager is only an extension of you: when a manager books you through an agent *you* pay the agent's commission; when a manager hires a publicity agent for you *you* pay for it; when a manager flies to L.A. to talk to people in the music biz *you* pay for the trip. Don't get this point confused. Managers pay for nothing but their own office overhead. This is one reason why managers always have more money than you do.

2. Deals with managers usually begin somewhat tentatively. The manager agrees to handle your affairs and to pursue a recording contract for your band in return for a percentage of your weekly gross. The contract will, of course, be written from the manager's point of view, and clause after clause will be devoted to protecting his or her position. It will usually have an initial term of one year, with options (management's, naturally) to renew. You should add to the contract anything you feel is needed to protect your position. For this reason you should have the contract checked out by an experienced entertainment lawyer (this will cost money unless you can find a friend or relative to arrange a favor). The band should have the option, for example, to cancel the contract if the manager has been unable to secure a recording contract in one year.

3. Beware of managers who try to tie up your performance, recording, and publishing rights into one huge five- to ten-year contractual deal out of which they take 25 percent or more from day one. This is asking too much from a new band—unless the manager is a nationally prominent "star" manager; even then you should look very hard at such a proposition.

4. Be suspicious of a manager who demands a high percentage cut (over 10 percent) while your gross receipts are still meager (under $2,000) a week. Managers should have to earn higher percentages by producing higher grosses. A sliding scale is usually a fair solution:

Your week's gross	*Management's cut*
$0–2,000	10%
$2,000–3,000	15%
$3,000–8,000	20%
$8,000 and above	25%

5. Check out prospective managers thoroughly. Do some detective work. Talk to anyone you can find who ever worked with them. Get an honest assessment of their strengths and weaknesses. If, for example, a band had a falling out with a manager you're interested in, find out why. You'll save yourself plenty of grief if you do your digging beforehand.

6. Delay signing the contract. If you wish, start working with a new manager under the terms of the contract, but don't sign it until the last possible moment. If things go wrong later, you will be the big loser, because the contract binds your services to the manager, *but not the manager's to you.* After signing, the only way you will be able to escape working through this manager is to strike; once you've signed, dealing with someone else—even making your own deals—can constitute breach of contract and grounds for a lawsuit. Most contracts specifically state that managers are "not required to render exclusive services" to *you*—in other words, they can let a band rot if they so desire. So I feel your band is morally justified in demanding (or even contriving) a trial period. You've proved that you can perform. Has your manager? Take a while to find out.

AGREEMENT made as of this 2nd day of December, 1974, between George W. Heath, 64 Winslow Ave. Somerville, Ma., John S. Macy, 35 Tower Rd. Lexington, Ma., Bill Henderson, 44 Magazine St. Cambridge, Ma., David Kinsman, 44 Magazine St. Cambridge, Ma., Kevin J. Lillis, 204 N. Harvard Ave. Allston, Ma., John D. McDonald, 122 Montgomery St. N. Cambridge, Ma.,. and John Lincoln Wright, 327 Allston St. Cambridge, Ma., (hereinafter referred to as "Artist") and Bruce Fink Productions Inc., P. O. Box 10, Cohasset, Ma. 02025 (hereinafter referred to as "Manager").

WHEREAS Artist wishes to obtain advice, guidance, counsel and direction in the development and furtherance of Artist's career as a performing artist, musician, composer, writer, and in such new and different areas (whether related or unrelated) as Artist's artistic talents can be developed and exploited, and

WHEREAS Manager by reason of Manager's contacts, experience and background, is qualified to render such advice, guidance, counsel and direction to Artist;

NOW, THEREFORE, in consideration of the mutual promises herein set forth, Artist and Manager agree:

1. Manager shall render such advice, guidance, counsel and other services as Artist may reasonably require to further Artist's career as a performing artist, musician, composer, and writer, and to develop new and different areas within which Artist's artistic talents can be developed and exploited, including but not limited to the following services:

    (a) to represent Artist and act as Artist's negotiator, to fix the terms governing all manner of disposition, use, employment or exploitation of Artist's talents and the products thereof;

    (b) to supervise Artist's professional employment and, on Artist's behalf, to consult with employers and prospective employers so as to assure the proper use and continued demand for Artist's services;

    (c) to be available at reasonable times and places to confer with Artist in connection with all matters concerning Artist's professional career, business interests, employment and publicity;

    (d) to exploit Artist's personality in all media, and in connection therewith to approve and permit for the purpose of trade, advertising and publicity, the use, dissemination, reproduction or publication of Artist's name, photographic likeness, voice and artistic and musical materials;

    (e) to engage, discharge and direct such theatrical agents, booking agencies, and employment agencies as well as other firms, persons or corporations who may be retained for the purpose of securing contracts, engagements or employment for Artist. It is understood, however, that Manager is not a booking agent but rather shall represent Artist in Artist's dealings with such agencies;

    (f) to represent Artist in all dealings with unions; and
    (g) to exercise all powers granted to Manager pursuant to Paragraph 4 of this agreement.

2. Manager is not required to render exclusive services to Artist or to devote Manager's entire time or the entire time of any of Manager's employees to Artist's affairs. Nothing herein shall be construed as limiting Manager' right to represent other persons whose talents may be similar to or who may be in competition with Artist or to have and pursue business interests which may be similar to or may compete with those of Artist.

3. Artist hereby appoints Manager as Artist's sole personal manager in all matters usually and normally within the jurisdiction and authority of personal managers, including but not limited to the advice, guidance, counsel and direction specifically referred to in Paragraph 1 hereof. Artist shall seek such advice, guidance, counsel and direction from Manager exclusively; shall not engage any other agent, representative or manager to render similar services; and shall not negotiate, accept or execute any agreement, understanding or undertaking concerning Artist's career without Manager's express prior consent.

4. Artist hereby irrevocably appoints Manager for the term of this agreement and any extensions hereof as Artist's true and lawful attorney-in-fact, to sign, make, execute and deliver all contracts in Artist's name; to make, execute, accept, endorse, collect and deliver all bills of exchange, checks and notes as Artist's said attorney; to demand, sue for, collect, recover, and receive all goods, claims, money, interest or other items that may be due to Artist or belong to Artist; and to make, execute and deliver receipts, releases or other discharges therfor, under sale or otherwise, and to defend, settle, adjust, submit to arbitration and compromise all actions, accounts, claims and demands which are or shall hereafter be pending, in such manner as Manager in Manager's sole discretion shall deem advisable; and without limiting the foregoing, generally to do, execute and perform any other act, deed or thing whatsoever that reasonably ought to be done, executed and performed, as fully and effectively as Artist could do if personally present; and Artist hereby ratifies and affirms all acts performed by Manager by virtue of this power of attorney.

Artist expressly agrees that Artist will not exert any of the powers herein granted to Manager by the foregoing power of attorney without the express prior written consent of Manager, and that all sums and considerations paid to Artist by reason of Artist's artistic endeavors shall be paid to Manager on behalf of Artist.

It is expressly understood that the foregoing power of attorney is limited to matters reasonably related to Artist's career as a performing artist, musician, composer, and writer, and such new and different areas within which Artist's artistic talents can be developed and exploited.

Artist understands and acknowledges that the power of attorney granted to Manager is coupled with an interest on Manager's part in the career of Artist, in the artistic talents or Artist, and in the products of that career and those talents and the earnings of Artist, arising by reason of such career, talents and products. Such power is therefore acknowledged by Artist to be irrevocable during the term of this agreement.

5. (a)   As compensation for services to be rendered hereunder, Manager shall receive from Artist (or shall retain from Artist's gross earnings) at the end of each calendar___week___ during the term hereof a sum of money equal to* _____ Percent (%) of Artist's gross earnings. Artist hereby assigns to Manager an interest in such earnings to the extent of _____ _____ Percent (%) hereof.

(b)   The term "gross earnings," as used herein, refers to the total of all earnings, which shall not be accumulated or averaged whether in the form of salary, bonuses, royalties (or advances against royalties), interests, percentages, shares of profits, merchandise, shares in ventures, products, properties, or any other kind or type of income which is reasonably related to Artist's career in the entertainment, amusement, music, recording, motion picture, television, radio, literary, theatrical and advertising fields and all similar areas whether now known or hereafter devised, in which Artist's artistic talents are developed and exploited, received by Artist or by any of Artist's heirs, executors, administrators, assigns, or by any person, firm or corporation (including Manager) on Artist's behalf.

(c)   The compensation agreed to be paid to Manager shall be based upon the gross earnings (as herein defined) of Artist accruing to or received by Artist during the term of this agreement or subsequent to the termination of this agreement as a result of any services performed by Artist during the term hereof or as the result of any contract negotiated during the term hereof and any renewal, extension or modification of such contract.

(i)   In the event that Manager accepts such offer, then the gross earnings of such corporation prior to the deduction of any corporate income taxes and of any corporate expenses or other deductions shall be included as part of Artist's gross earnings as herein defined, and any salary paid to Artist by such corporation shall be excluded from Artist's gross earnings for the purpose of calculating the compensation due to Manager hereunder.

* See Rider

(ii)   In the event Manager refuses such offer, then the gross earnings of such corporation (prior to deduction of all corporate income taxes, corporate expenses and all other deductions) shall be excluded from Artist's gross earnings as defined hereunder, and such salary as is paid to Artist by such corporation shall be included as part of Artist's gross earnings as herein defined.

(e)   In the event that during the term hereof Artist forms a corporation or enters into a contract with a corporation for the purpose of exploiting or furnishing Artist's artistic talents, then in addition to all other consideration to be paid to Manager hereunder, Manager shall be entitled to purchase at least _____Twenty Five_____ Percent (25%) of the capital stock of such corporation at the same price as such stock is initially offered to the other stockholders. Artist shall not enter into any contract with a corporation or create a corporation for such purpose unless such option is made available to Manager.

(f)   Artist's gross earnings as herein defined shall be paid directly to Manager by all persons, firms or corporations, and Manager may withhold his compensation therefrom and may reimburse himself therefrom for any fees, costs or expenses advanced or incurred by Manager pursuant to Paragraph 6 hereof. In the event that Artist nevertheless receives gross earnings directly, Artist shall be deemed to hold in trust for Manager that portion of Artist's gross earnings which equals Manager's compensation hereunder and such disbursements incurred by Manager on behalf of Artist.

6. Artist shall be solely responsible for payment of all booking agencies' fees, union dues, publicity costs, promotion or exploitation costs, travelling expenses and wardrobe expenses. In the event that Manager advances any of the foregoing fees, costs or expenses on behalf of Artist, or incurs any other reasonable expenses in connection with Artist's professional career or with the performance of Manager's services hereunder, Artist shall promptly reimburse Manager for such fees, costs and expenses.

7. Artist represents and warrants that Artist is under no disability, restriction or prohibition with respect to Artist's right to execute this agreement and perform its terms and conditions. Artist warrants and represents that no act or omission by Artist hereunder will violate any right or interest of any person or firm or will subject Manager to any liability, or claim of liability to any person. Artist hereby agrees to indemnify Manager and to hold Manager harmless against any damages, costs, expenses, fees (including attorneys' fees) incurred by Manager in any claim, suit or proceeding instituted against Manager and arising out of any breach or claimed breach by Artist of any warranty,

representation or covenant of Artist's. Artist shall exert Artist's best efforts to further Artist's professional career during the term of this agreement and Artist shall cooperate with Manager to the fullest extent in the interest of promoting Artist's career.

8. The initial term of this agreement shall be for a period of ___One (1)___ year commencing with the date first indicated above. Manager shall have the irrevocable option to renew this agreement for _Three (3)_ additional periods of __One (1)__ year each by written notice mailed to Artist no less than thirty (30) days prior to the expiration of the then-current term of this agreement.

9. Manager shall maintain accurate books and records of all transactions concerning Artist, which books and records may be inspected by a certified public accountant designated by Artist, upon reasonable notice to Manager, at Manager's office in Massachusetts during regular business hours.

10. As a condition precedent to any assertion by Artist or Manager that the other is in default in performing any obligation contained herein, the party alleging the default must advise the other in writing of the specific facts upon which it is claimed that the other is in default and of the specific obligation which it is claimed has been breached, and the other party shall be allowed a period of sixty (60) days after receipt of such written notice within which to cure such default. During such period, no breach of any obligation shall be deemed to be incurable.

11. This agreement represents the entire understanding between the parties and can only be modified or amended by a written document signed by the party sought to be charged. This agreement shall be construed in accordance with the law of the State of New York applicable to agreements executed and to be wholly performed therein, and shall be binding upon and inure to the benefit of the parties' respective heirs, executors, administrators, successors and assigns.

12. Any controversy or claim arising out of or relating to this agreement, or breach hereof, shall be settled by arbitration held in Massachusetts in accordance with the Rules of the American Arbitration Association, and judgment upon the award rendered by the Arbitrator(s) may be entered in any court having jurisdiction thereof.

13. In the event any provision hereof shall for any reason be illegal or unenforceable, the same shall not affect the validity or enforceability of the remaining provisions hereof.

IN WITNESS THEREOF, the parties hereto have executed this agreement as of the day and year first indicated above.

_____

Artist

_____

Artist

_____

Artist

_____

Artist

_____

Artist

_____

Manager

RIDER to Agreement made as of the 2nd day of December, 1974, between ••••, (hereinafter referred to as "Artist") and ••••••, (hereinafter referred to as "Manager").

1. Notwithstanding the provisions of Paragraph 5 (a), in the event Artist's gross earnings with respect to any week of the term hereof are less than Fifteen Hundred Dollars ($1500.00), the Manager shall be entitled to receive compensation in the amount of Ten Percent (10%) of such gross earnings. If such gross earnings during any week are between Fifteen Hundred Dollars ($1500.00) and Twenty Five Hundred Dollars ($2500.00), the aforesaid compensation shall be Fifteen Percent (15%) with respect to all gross earnings during such week. If such gross earnings during any week are between Twenty Five Hundred Dollars ($2500.00) and Seventy Five Hundred Dollars ($7500.) the applicable compensation shall be Twenty Percent (20%) with respect to all gross earnings during any such week. If such gross earnings during any week of the term exceeded Seventy Five Hundred Dollars ($7500.00), Manager shall be entitled to receive compensation in the amount of Twenty Five Percent (25%).

2. It is acknowledged by Artist that in addition to those activities referred to in Paragraph 2 of the Agreement, Manager is actively involved in other aspects of the entertainment industry. Such involvement shall continue during the term hereof and shall not be raised as a basis for any claim of non-performance of this Agreement by the Manager.

3. The Manager agrees that he will devote a reasonable amount of time necessary for the proper explotation and promo-

tion of the Artist's performing abilities and that if at the end of
one year after the date of Agreement Manager has not secured
a recording contract or entered into negotiations with a major
recording company then the Artist will have the right to cancel
the option to renew this Agreement; or to renegotiate the terms
of the option.

BEWARE

If you've begun to think about management and wish you had a hot-
shot manager, you may be ripe for making a hasty decision. Here is a
list of cautionary thoughts that you may find useful:

1. Unless the results are prompt and impressive (which they
rarely are), it's hard to measure the manager's immediate value to
your band. Crooked managers can steal from you easily; lazy managers can let things slide for quite a while before it becomes obvious
that they aren't putting in their time; sloppy managers can let your
affairs fall into disarray and you won't know about it for months. All
of these situations are violations of the trust you must put in them,
because you can't watch them all the time. To monitor your manager takes as much time as doing things yourself, so if you find yourself having to do so, my advice is to drop the manager.

2. Avoid flashy businessmen, club owners, or media personalities who want to "manage" you in their spare time. They may gen-
uinely appreciate your ability, but their desire to manage is often
unrealistic and escapist. If they're really successful at what they're
doing, they will probably be bad managers—at least as far as you're
concerned. They're too busy with their real work to give your business the time it needs.

3. Make sure that your manager's personality is compatible with
your own. Remember that a manager *represents* you; if your manager
is not presentable in manner and reasonable in style, you're keeping
bad company.

4. If your manager isn't a close friend to begin with, don't try to
establish a deep personal relationship. It's a business deal; you might
forget it, but you can bet your manager won't. Cordiality with emotional distance is the best stance. Otherwise you'll be less ready to
challenge irregularities that come up. You have to be on guard with
a manager. If things are too friendly you won't be able to keep your
eye on your affairs without feeling guilty.

5. Managers can come from all sorts of backgrounds, but on
inspection, most of them share certain kinds of experience. Prac-

tically all of them have done time in some end of the music industry, either as a musician or in one of the allied businesses. This means they are not outsiders when they start to manage; they have friends and contacts throughout the business that they can begin to use for their own (and your) benefit.

A good manager's background might look something like this: a former musician with several years' experience in a major booking agency. What you don't want to see is a former actor and dope dealer with experience as a rock journalist.

6. During your shakedown period with a manager, don't be shy. Voice your suspicions and doubts; ask what is being done for you. If the report is vague and unspecified, don't be afraid to demand more details. Beware of evasiveness: if a manager seems impatient with having to talk to you or can't really come up with many concrete examples of what's being done for the band, you should press for more information.

A favorite trick of a manager up a tree is to recite a long list of phone calls that have been made for you, hoping that this will sound like lots of hard work and make you feel guilty for asking. Well, anyone can *make* a phone call. That, in itself, is nothing. Ask: What were the results? Have all the phone calls been followed up with a confirmation call or a letter? Are the others scheduled for follow-ups? And so on. Who hasn't been called, and why? Look for results. What have all those phone calls *produced?* A manager must be accountable to you; that's the only way you're going to know whether the job is being done.

7. Beware of managers who seem to be working with too many bands. Collecting that 10 to 15 percent of every week's gross can become such a comfortable living that managers are tempted to load up on the number of bands they handle, beyond their capacity to really handle them. Such a situation will produce nothing but anger and frustration for you as you watch your manager miss booking opportunities, neglect to follow up on solid possibilities, book you into completely inappropriate clubs, and generally seem to ignore you for long periods of time.

DO YOU NEED A MANAGER?

Here's a summary of my admittedly biased attitudes: unless you're seasoned and ready to shoot for your record deal (give yourselves a minimum of one to two years to develop), you don't need a manager unless (1) you've proved yourself incompetent to carry out your basic business responsibilities, (2) you hate business so much that you're all having nervous breakdowns, or (3) there is so much business to do that you have no time left for music.

If you don't want to get into a complex management relationship yet you might look for someone who can help you part-time, doing, say, your books and secretarial work. Eventually the arrangement could expand into routine booking chores, if things work out. This kind of limited business relationship often acts as a stopgap, allowing you to coast on your own steam until the day comes when you absolutely must join forces with a full-time manager.

You may *never* need a manager. Many working bands survive and thrive for years without one. If you read this book you'll know enough to avoid managers for a while. Remember, they take 10 to 25 percent off the top of your gross. There will be weeks your manager will make more than any one of you makes!

THE UNION

Many musicians wonder if they can gain benefits by joining their local musicians union. The best advice I ever got on the matter of union membership is: don't join the union until you absolutely have to. In all but a few locales the union (American Federation of Musicians) is rarely a factor in anything a new rock 'n' roll band does. You will know it's time to join when you are told, flatly, that in order to work where you want to work, you must be a union band.

The union does not obtain work for your band. If you are union members you are forbidden to work with nonunion musicians. As a union member you are not allowed to work in nonunion clubs. The initiation fee can be as high as several hundred dollars; then come your union dues, payable quarterly—and, of course, when you work the union takes a percentage of your gross pay, in the form of "work dues."

What do you get out of this? If you're a young band, just starting to work, you'll be hard-pressed to think of any way the union can really be of much help to you. Most clubs pay something close to minimum scale anyway, so you don't need the union to enforce that for you. Unless the union local in your area is extremely strong, the clubs where you'll get your start are not under union control; thus, by "Catch-22," join the union and you won't be able to get your start. If you're interested in pension and death benefits, the union has programs that might attract you, as well as legal services (although they are slow and bureaucratic).

The union's history is honorable, and I don't want to knock the contributions it has made in the working life of the average professional musician. It's just that on the teeming and swarming lower levels of rock 'n' roll, the union has little to offer.

17

THE RECORD DEAL

I f you are close to making a major recording deal, you've probably outgrown any advice I can give you. But bands can be "close to a deal" for years. This is the purgatory of the regionally successful band: they seem to be so popular around home that it's hard to understand why they haven't been picked up by a major label. The reasons are not always obvious; they have a lot to do with the direction of trends inside the music industry and with general economic conditions. In the late 1960s, for example, homegrown bands seemed to be the salvation of the industry; it was easy to get signed. In the '70s the stakes rose; corporate control became tighter, with a tendency to enhance the careers of already established performers and avoid taking chances on new bands. In the '80s some new trends got a little bit of air (rap, new wave, etc.) but radio formats became rigid (favoring the few rather than the many). As for video, if you weren't on MTV, you could hardly be said to exist. These trends continue into the '90s, along with some interesting growth of independent label potential, particularly in the rap and alternative areas. The bottom line? It's devilishly hard to get signed.

WHY RECORD?

If you want to play concerts rather than clubs, to open for big-name artists, or to tour, you will have to deal with powerful national and regional booking agencies. They won't even talk to you if you haven't made (or are in the process of concluding) a record deal. It's not in their interest to do so; they have no need whatsoever for unknown acts who lack the promotional leverage of an album in the stores.

157

Having an album out won't absolutely insure good work for you, but it will qualify you to enter the "national" scene—at the fringes, most likely, but national nonetheless—where with luck, tenacity, hard work, two or three more albums, and a couple of years on the road, you stand a chance of rising to respectable prominence. The album, in a nutshell, makes you "legitimate," just as a college diploma is supposed to "qualify" you to enter certain job markets.

More important, the album is a promotional tool, a catalyst that allows a nexus of club owners, promoters, recording-business people, and radio and print media to make some money off of you. Getting you out to be seen is to their definite advantage, as long as there's an album to tie all their efforts together. But with no album you are as good as nonexistent to these people.

If you want to operate at the national level, a major recording contract is ultimately what you're after. Unfortunately, there is no reliable or predictable process that will ensure you get it. There are, however, certain steps you must follow before you even qualify—and ways you might expect your deal to come about.

THE DEMO

It used to be said that you shouldn't worry about sending a humble basement tape to a record company: they would hear the potential if it was there. I never believed it, and if it was ever true, it certainly isn't true today. I pointed out in chapter 10 that for "record bait" you would need a very special, well-produced demo tape; you are competing head-on with lots of bands as good as you are, if not better. The bald fact is that a shabby-sounding demo will only get you into the wastebasket.

Now your tape should showcase your original material. If no one in the band writes, you should find someone who does. Record companies will be far less interested in you if you lack original material. You need no more than two, possibly three numbers. Each cut should be produced as carefully as if you were recording a single for release.

Needless to say, everything should be rehearsed and worked out to the last beat before you go into the studio; and the studio you choose should be the best you can find. At this stage it might be wise to bring in an experienced producer. But make sure you know who you're working with and respect his or her work—and that this producer understands and respects what you do. Quality production will be tough to afford, but do the best you can. Going for a recording deal deserves your best shot.

APPROACHING THE DEAL

It takes more than a good tape to get the wheels rolling. Several things should be happening at once.

1. Someone should be wheeling and dealing for you. You must be professionally represented, and your representative must be regularly in touch with the men and women who acquire new talent for the major record companies: producers, executives, A&R reps. Of all people, they are in the best position to start some action.

2. Reports must be coming in from your region that you are an excellent local draw and that you maintain a substantial and growing following. Your name should have filtered up to executive level in the home offices in New York, L.A., Nashville, Detroit, or wherever. This process can be accelerated by clever, promotion-minded management.

3. You must be seen. If a major label is interested in you they'll look at you a number of times before they make any commitment. The top executives ultimately decide who gets signed. If you have a champion in the lower echelons of the company it doesn't necessarily mean you'll get your deal. But it's a good omen. Sometimes, if you don't have a proper demo, an A&R rep or house producer will arrange for you to make a tape at the label's expense. That's progress. Showcase gigs are sometimes arranged: the label throws you on as opener to one of their acts or arranges an appearance at a showcase club in the home-office city. If the company is serious they might fly some executives out to see you on your home turf.

4. You must be functioning intelligently, and with a plan, rather than leaving things up to chance. A band isn't simply "discovered." Rather, it plays an intricate and extended game (the process would make an excellent board game!) with strategy, rules, timing, and skill. The bands with the greatest understanding of how to play this game have a tremendous advantage over their competitors.

Don't expect things to happen overnight. Just as it took time to establish yourselves locally, it will take time to establish the band as a bona-fide candidate for a recording contract. Four or five years is an average time span, from inception to contract, for the successful band. Success, like other things of value, takes its time coming.

WHO MAKES THE DEAL?

There is big money to be made in the record business, so it draws tough, quick, streetwise types who, given ten seconds, can think of ten different ways to make money off a business deal coming and going. Because at least five of these ways will involve placing themselves between some talent and whoever wants that talent, you'll encounter all sorts of go-betweens on your search for the deal.

An enterprising independent producer may want to sign you to a production deal, assuring you, in return, a contract with this or that major label. A publisher who is interested in your original songs may want to sign you to a publishing agreement that involves a recording contract. A national booking agency can get that elusive recording deal for you—provided they're convinced of your potential drawing power; but they won't do it unless they get a piece of the deal they help you make (everyone will want a piece of your deal, meaning a percentage of your royalties). The cleverest of all, in a way, are the pure facilitators (nearly always lawyers) who step between your manager and *everything* else, arranging a package involving recording, publishing, and booking, none of which they are directly involved in, except to pull out their piece of each slice of the pie.

All this is very complex and financially hazardous. You won't want to sail these rough waters without solid business and legal representation. You must have implicit confidence in your manager, or whoever is doing the talking for you, and you must have the services of a lawyer who's familiar with the ins and outs of the record business.

Sadly enough, you can't expect a fair deal from a major company until you've won a measure of respect; if you and your people refuse to let them walk all over you they'll pick up the signals and stop trying to skin you in the obvious ways. The major label folks don't exactly get up in the morning trying to see how evil they can be; it's just that they are compulsive power players. When it comes down to putting a contract on the table (their contract, their table), they will, without malice, try to win every piece on the board in their first move. Don't be shocked; this is merely standard. Now it's your move. Take the contract to your lawyer and make all the changes you want. It'll go back and forth many times before there's an agreement.

Going for a recording contract has always been an arduous trek, and as we approach the end of the century, with competition growing, it's even harder than ever to get "discovered." The major labels have been gobbled up by giant international conglomerates, and are run by corporate flunkies who want their butts covered at all times. This limits the signings of new talent. There are fewer ways a new band can break through. The trends of the '60s and early '70s toward free-format FM radio were quickly overcome by preprocessed formats, featuring small, preselected playlists. (Think about it: How many bands get exposure on MTV in a given week? How many MTVs are there?) There is nothing today like the concert-style rock ballrooms in which most of the bands of the '60s cut their teeth. Established clubs that specialize in showcasing new talent are few and far between—and not increasing in number.

In other words, avenues of exposure are actually decreasing. This has two major implications: (1) your band, ready as it might be for the country to take notice, must survive a drastic selection process that leaves many good bands unselected, unrecorded, unseen, and ultimately out of business; and (2), in a time when money is tighter, recording companies are forced to spend more to "break" a new band; naturally, they'll take on fewer new acts.

So we're all victims of history: your band, because you may not get the shot you deserve; record companies, because they can't afford to experiment; and the public, because they may never even hear you or other bands they might have liked.

A sane perspective on all this is to put away your dreams of overnight success and decide that you are in for the long haul. The main business of this book is to help you keep working and taking the kinds of steps that will upgrade your working situation locally and regionally. If the major record companies are not falling all over your doorstep, it's no cause for alarm. However, with a firm local following and spreading regional popularity, you are nonetheless in a position to give yourself a firm push by getting an album out.

IN THE GROOVES AT LAST

In response to this dismal situation for unknown bands, an interesting phenomenon is developing: as the major record companies find themselves less and less able to take advantage of smallish markets for regionally popular bands or new musical trends, independent companies are jumping in to service this need. What it means is that you can sign for a one-shot deal with, say, "Big Toe Records," who will record you and distribute and promote your album through selective channels.

Advantages to Working with an Independent Label versus Major Labels or Going on Your Own

1. You will get next to no airplay by circulating your own cassette copy of your demo. Many stations will not play anything that's

not on record or CD. Being on disk gives you credibility, to the radio people: it makes you "real."

2. With an album out on a bona-fide label, minor though it is, you have at least some of the legitimacy conferred on "recorded" bands. The album can be used for radio promotion; record stores that carry it might even feature it in an ad if they feel your popularity is solid enough to draw customers. You'll be seen and heard more often and by more people as a result of the album—even if these people never actually see or hear the album itself!

3. The album can become a part of your own promotion kit. Its public-relations value is immense and practically endless. Everyone you deal with (or would like to be in touch with) will be happy to receive a copy of the album, and it's a good excuse to renew old contacts and make new ones.

4. Friendly local record stores will sometimes push the album as a sentimental favorite—and that's free promotion!

5. You'll find that you're able to sell a few at every gig. Carry them around and tell the crowd they're available at each break.

6. And yes, there is always the chance that your album will take off. You might find a radio personality who likes it well enough to put a cut or two on the playlist. If you spin out a regional hit, program directors of larger stations might take a chance on it. A couple of monster hits every year start out this way. If this happens you're bound to end up with what you wanted all along: the major recording contract.

DO IT YOURSELF

What if the small independent labels are too specialized for your purposes (blues only, bluegrass and country, new wave, rap, etc.) or run by characters with whom you'd just rather not do business? If you can't find a company that seems to suit your style, you might consider putting out your own 7-inch EP or full-length CD/cassette. Many recording studios will be glad to take on this process, which involves preparing master tapes and sending them off to a manufacturer who will turn out as many copies of the end product as you order. You can take your tapes to the manufacturer yourself—it will bring you one step closer to the process. But if you trust your studio, you might as well let them handle the inevitable hassles; they're probably more knowledgeable than you and will see the process through without significantly more expense. The total tab will run anywhere from $500 to $1,000 or so, depending on whom you deal with and how large your order (you can always reorder if you need more).

The advantage of doing it yourself is that, because you've paid for the whole thing, you get every cent back on a sale. Of course, this is only true if you sell it personally; you'll give up sizable percentages once record stores start handling it or if you place it with a distributor. Even so, your take-home share will still always be greater, because you'd start by giving away a flat 50 percent per copy on your small-label deal. Bottom line: if the do-it-yourself album takes off, you stand to make considerably more money than if a record company had put it out.

Four Reasons *Not* to Produce Your Own Recordings

1. Your large initial cash outlay, which is never easy to raise

2. Your comparative lack of technical experience in the record biz

3. Your lack of distribution channels

4. Your limited amount of time and money for promotion. Even a small record company is in the business of making and promoting albums full-time, which is more time than you have available.

The ultimate truth, no matter who handles the job, or on what level, is that it means a lot for you to be "in print." You should always keep the possibility of putting the band on record or CD somewhere in the back of your mind. When the time is ripe—perhaps now it's too soon—take a shot at it in one way or another. Don't act hastily; give the band a chance to mature. This could take anywhere from six months to a couple of years, depending on how much experience everyone had at the start. But after a certain point producing an album is the logical move to make.

APPEARANCES CREATE SALES

Finally, it's impossible to stress how important it is for the band to get out and work—to be seen—to complement an album's release. This is true on any level. Album sales and personal appearances support each other. By carefully planning around the release of an album, you can increase the number of copies sold. This rule holds equally true for you as it does for the top touring bands (always on tour, if you notice, behind the release of a new album). It's appropriate to close this final chapter in the middle of a reminder to keep working. Work is really the essential factor in any band's success or failure. When the Beatles stopped working their days as a band were numbered. The same thing will happen to you. So be a working band! Just remember, as you move into the territory ahead: keep your eyes wide open and watch where you swim: those glittering waters are full of sharks.

BREAKING UP

Like the song says, breaking up is hard to do—not to mention discouraging—even if it relieves a lot of long-term tensions. It's a trauma. Bands have a way of avoiding the notion of breaking up, so that when it happens (as it does someday to all bands) it's messy and mutually abusive. This need not be.

First, some breakups are needless and premature. Don't make the mistake of chucking everything when the signs indicate you're only six months away from good money and good work. Sometimes a decision to disband hides a fear of confronting your problems head-on—and solving them *without* breaking up. Get your reasons straight and think over all the alternatives.

Take some time off

Maybe everyone is suffering from a case of "band fatigue" (see chapter 14). Consider a good long vacation—a month or six weeks—and plan to talk it over again when everyone's had some rest. The effectiveness of time off is something you have to take on faith: it works.

Changes of personnel

Conflicts of personality or musical direction may have brought you to the breaking point. More difficult is a case of one band member whose skills are decaying. It takes courage to face this situation, to fire somebody, and to stand up and assume that kind of responsibility. But if the band is worth saving, and the pain is great enough, you'll discover a great relief in taking this step. As ugly as things might get for a week or two, the ugliness and bad feeling will wash away pretty quickly, leaving the band ready to tap new energy.

Make some big changes

Changes in material may sometimes redirect the course of a band's development in a positive direction. Adding a new instrument—keyboards or a horn, for example—can change your outlook. Adding a new lead vocalist can transform a band, especially if you are weak in this department. Egos suffer whenever someone is moved out of the spotlight, but this is part of everyone's growing process and should not be considered an insurmountable barrier to vital changes.

A CLEAN BREAK

But breaking up is often unavoidable, and sometimes the right thing to do. When this is the case, it should be done cleanly and graciously on everyone's part. Certain amenities should be held to scrupulously.

1. Don't screw anybody financially. If the band is carrying debts, plan to keep working until the debts are paid. Because loan contracts or finance papers will most likely be in the name of one of the band members, that person will be legally liable for the debt. Don't leave your benefactor holding the bag. This, by the way, is another reason not to be in a state of heavy debt—it makes it very difficult to break up!

2. Sell all communal property and divide the money (providing it doesn't get eaten up by band debts). Sometimes it's difficult to determine a way of dividing things up that is both exact and totally satisfactory to everyone. Try not to hassle too much over the money—it will only leave a bitter taste in everyone's mouth. If each band member gets approximately what's coming, let it go at that. The few bucks you will gain, or someone else will forfeit, is not worth the bad will. This is a time to go easy.

3. Sometimes an important band member's resignation triggers the demise of the band. If this is inevitable, try to avoid hostile feelings toward that individual. Everyone has a personal life to take care of, as well as the life of the band, and you're kidding yourself if you feel resentment toward someone for making a life decision on personal terms.

This is a time for understanding all around, not bad feelings. Keep in touch with your old mates because new opportunities form from the wreckage of old bands. And, like it or not, you've shared a chunk of your life with each other. To deny the experience, to write the whole thing off with bad feeling, is to deny that portion of your life. Remember all the intensely good moments, as well as the bad times, and respect them all. Saying goodbye is not an occasion for pettiness.

CONCLUSION

Bands are not immortal. They have a lifespan, but that lifespan can be increased and made more productive if, from the start, you know what to do—and go out and do it. That's what this book is about and I hope the information is useful to you.

I'm not a manager or an agent, and I never intend to be; that's why this book displays an almost total bias toward the musician and against anyone who might hurt the musician. If I've been hard on the pure-business types in music, I regret the need to be so, but any experienced musician has been mistreated enough times to be eternally on guard when doing business with anybody. I've tried to transfer some of this caution to these pages without disguising the fact that this book is for you, the musician, and for anyone else who is interested in sharing the musician's perspective. I hope it has served you well. And, wherever you want your band to go, I hope you go all the way. Just don't forget to have fun!

glossary

A&R: the "artists and repertoire" department of a major record label. A&R people formerly helped find material for artists under contract to the label. Today their job is to scout promising new artists for the label.

agent: anyone in the business of making connections between artists and gigs. The kind you'll most often deal with is a "booking agent," whose job is to represent you in negotiations with those who may want to hire you. Often booking agents have "exclusive" booking arrangements with certain clubs, which makes them the "gatekeepers" to those clubs. They know every game in town and play them all. But you've got to love 'em: they get you work.

amp head: the portion of any amplifier system that contains the electronics (tubes, solid state circuitry, etc.) and the controls. Sometimes it is included with the speakers in a single box; sometimes it is a separate component.

Cannon connectors: multiprong plugs and receptors, often used in PA systems to make mike-cable-amplifier connections.

changes: sequences of chords, like E-A-B7-E, etc. Called "modulations" by classical musicians.

contract rider: any addition to a standard contract to cover a special circumstance. If free lodging is part of your deal, for instance, this should be added to your contract in a rider.

crossover: a song rearranged and performed in a style different from its original category. It literally "crosses over" from one category to another. Example: a C&W hit that you reinterpret as a heavy-metal rocker.

cue mix: in a recording session, a special mix, for the players, heard through headphones. A good cue mix is customized so that each player can hear his or her own instrument.

cutoff: a strong hand signal from one of the performers to "cut off" a held chord (usually the last chord of a song). Elaborate cutoffs can often laced with showmanship (the leap in the air, the flamboyant swipe with a guitar neck), but their principal purpose is musical.

demo: a recording made for limited "demonstration" purposes, i.e., to represent your work to an agent, club owner, radio station, etc.

door (as in "the door"): the admission fee collected at the entrance to a club or other pay-as-you-enter event.

dub: a tape that is a copy of a "master" recording. Dubs are usually run off in multiple batches.

flyer: a printed, one-page advertisement for your band. It can be for general use ("Available for clubs, concerts, parties") or to promote a specific event ("At the Music Barn, Aug. 4–7").

fuse: a safety device that breaks an electrical circuit if the load reaches danger point. In most of your equipment the fuse is a small glass tube, encased in metal at either end. House fuses screw into a house fuse box and look like the bottom of a light bulb (today most homes—and business establishments—use circuit breakers, which are simple reset switches, instead of fuses).

gig: slang for a job. It can be a specific date or a long-term engagement, even an ordinary job ("day gig").

guarantee: a set amount of money a club or other employer "guarantees" you "against the door"—meaning if your percentage of money collected at the door exceeds the guarantee, you'll make more—but by agreement, no less than the guarantee. Nice work if you can get it.

guide track: in a recording session, a "scratch" lead vocal, laid down by your vocalist, to "guide" the instrumentalists through recording their tracks. It will be replaced by a more polished final vocal track.

high impedance: without getting into electrical theory, the kind of circuit designed to connect instruments to their amps. Some rudimentary PA systems also utilize high-impedance circuits. Low-impedance circuits are used for more elaborate systems.

house fuse (see **fuse**): a safety device for use in a house electrical system that breaks a circuit when it's so overloaded the result could be heat and fire. Thus, when the lights blow out you generally need a new fuse—and to move some of your electrical load to a new circuit.

key change: when the home chord (or "I chord") changes. Going from a song in E to a song in G involves a key change. Key changes can also occur within a single song.

lead break: the instrumental solo section of a song.

leakage: when a band records in real time (as opposed to track by track) sound from one instrument can "leak" onto another instrument's track. For example: the mike set up to record the lead guitar "hears" spillover from the drums. Sound-absorbent barriers are usually positioned to minimize leakage.

level: a measure of loudness. Level controls on an amplifier or mixing board lower the volume (perceived loudness) of an instrument or vocal track.

manager: someone who agrees to handle the business end of your operation in exchange for a percentage of your income.

medley: a group of songs, usually by the same artist or in the same style, played (often in a shortened version) without breaks. Examples: a blues medley, a Rolling Stones medley.

mixdown: the final product of a recording session. All tracks are balanced and "mixed down" to a two-track stereo master.

mixer: a piece of equipment that allows you, or your sound person, to combine and balance various separate tracks of your sound.

monitor system: a separate sound mix, so that band members can hear themselves onstage. A "monitor mix" is sent back to speakers on the stage floor, positioned at the feet of each player.

partial payment: payment of only part of what you are owed. Often, partial payment is bait to tempt you to complete an engagement for which the employer has no intention of paying you the full amount.

PA column: a cluster of speakers designed to work with a PA system and enclosed in a rectangular, column-like cabinet.

PA system: the microphones, amp, mixer, and speakers you use to amplify the vocalists in your band—as well as (in elaborate systems) the instruments themselves.

per diem: when on the road, you'll need "walking around money." The per diem (it literally means "by the day" in Latin) is a set amount, usually in cash, advanced to each band member to cover food and other daily incidentals.

phone plug: the largest of the standard single-prong plug connectors. Usually the kind of plug that connects your instrument to your amp.

polarity: a characteristic of amps, as electrical systems, which can cause you to get electrical shocks. The remedy is to "reverse the polarity" by flicking the "ground" switch on your amp up (if it's down) or down (if it's up).

power tubes: in an amp, the great big tubes, which are most crucial to the amp's operation—and will leave you with dead air if they fail.

rhythm section: the segment of the band most concerned with the beat—giving it character and keeping it steady. Usually comprises the drummer, bass, and rhythm guitar player.

set screws: screws that hold components of a piece of equipment together.

snake: in low-impedance PA systems, a long cable combining the cords for each mike of a system, running from stage to the mixing panel, which is usually near the back of the room.

woodshedding: rehearsing privately for a period of time, to put your show together, improve your performance technically, or enhance your presentation.

select bibliography

BOOKS

There are a number of good books about the "high end" of the music business—that is, the New York–Los Angeles-based mega-world of big deals, contracts, super-managers, lawyers, major labels, and publishing companies that combine to form what's often called the music "industry." If your long-term ambitions tend toward the major recording contract, if you're serious about writing and promoting your own original material and collecting a Grammy someday, the following books will be a wealth of valuable information for you.

Brabec, Todd and Jeffrey. *Music, Money and Success.* New York: Schirmer Books, 1994. A good overview of the music industry written by two insiders.

Clevo, Jim, and Eric Olsen. *Networking in the Music Industry.* San Diego: Rock Press, 1994. A truly impressive compendium of first-hand information, from real people in every conceivable arena of the music business—and in their own words. Buy this one first.

Dannen, Fredric. *Hit Men.* New York: Vintage, 1991. Inside dirt. A must read.

Passman, Donald S. *All You Need to Know About the Music Business.* New York: Simon & Schuster, 1991, 1994. Again, mostly deals, agents, managers, publishers, record companies, etc.

Shemel, Sidney, and M. William Krasilovsky. *This Business of Music.* 6th ed. New York: Billboard, 1990. The industry bible: no need to own this exhaustive (and expensive) reference. Your library will most likely have it.

Siegel, Alan. *Breaking into the Music Business.* New York: Fireside/Simon & Schuster, 1973. Siegel is openly passionate (and a lawyer, at that!) in his desire to help you know what you need to know.

There are some good books for the workaday band musician, too. Here are a few.

Anderson, Craig. *Do-It-Yourself Projects for Guitarists.* San Francisco: Miller Freeman, 1994. "35 Useful, Inexpensive Electronic Projects to Help Unlock Your Instrument's Potential." For you guitar hot-rodders. Takes you all the way from how to read basic schematics to how to customize your ax—35 different ways!

Baker, Bob. *101 Ways Right Now to Make Money in the Music Business.* San Diego: Rock Press, 1992. "An A-Z guide to cashing in on your talents." Count 'em.

Baxter, Mark. *The Rock 'n' Roll Singer's Survival Manual.* Milwaukee: Hal Leonard, 1990. Singers, take care of those pipes! Here's how.

Weissman, Dick. *Making a Living in Your Local Music Market.* Milwaukee: Hal Leonard, 1990. A little of this, a little of that.

Right now there is a surprisingly large number of good books out on how to write and sell songs:

Gillette, Steve. *Songwriting and the Creative Process.* New York: Sing Out!, 1995.

Josefs, Jai. *Writing Music for Hit Songs.* New York: Schirmer Books, 1996. Focuses on the melody, harmony, and arrangement of all styles of popular music.

Luboff, Pat and Pete. *88 Songwriting Wrongs and How to Right Them.* Cincinnati: Writer's Digest Books, 1992.

Liggett, Mark and Cathy. *The Complete Handbook of Songwriting (An Insider's Guide to Making It in the Music Industry).* 2d ed. New York: Plume, 1993.

Pincus, Les. *The Songwriter's Success Manual.* New York: Music Press, 1974.

Want to go on the road? In line with the philosophy of my book, here's an indispensable guide to lining up your own gigs and planning sensible, low-cost travel.

Garo, Liz. *Book Your Own Tour.* San Diego: Rock Press, 1995. "The independent musician's guide to cost-effective touring and promotion."

Want to release your own record? Try these two titles:

Hustwit, Gary. *Releasing an Independent Record.* 5th ed. San Diego: Rock Press, 1995.

———. *Getting Radio Airplay.* 2d ed. San Diego: Rock Press, 1995. A guide to getting your music played on college, public, and commercial radio. Rock Press is distributed by Mix Bookshelf, which puts out a terrific catalogue of books covering every aspect of the music business. 6400 Hollis Street, #12 Emeryville, CA 94608, 800-233-9604.

Another treasure trove of books, instructional videos, tapes, and CDs is the Music Dispatch Catalog. Music Dispatch, P.O. Box 13920, Milwaukee, WI, 800-637-2852.

MAGAZINES

There are a number of good magazines that can be your guide to specific information about who's who, what's new, and "how to"— including brand names, interviews, playing tips, and song transcriptions. Certainly browsing through these magazines is one of the best ways to learn about the hardware of rock. A full-spectrum newsstand will stock most of these magazines. In case you have trouble finding them, I've included the subscription address (and don't forget that subscription prices are invariably more economical, issue for issue, than single-copy prices at the newsstand).

Bass Player
PO Box 57324
Boulder, CO 80322-7324

Electronic Musician
PO Box 8845
Emeryville, CA 94662-9947

Guitar
PO Box 53063
Boulder, CO 80323-3063

Guitar Player
800-289-9839
303-678-0439 (CO and outside the U.S.)

Guitar School
1115 Broadway
New York, NY 10160-0261

Guitar Shop: "The Only All-Gear Magazine"
PO Box 1490
Port Chester, NY 10573

Keyboard
PO box 50404
Boulder, CO 80323-0404

Modern Drummer
PO Box 480
Mt. Morris, IL 61054-0480

Musician
PO Box 1923
Marion, OH 43306-2023

Recording: "The Magazine for the Recording Musician."
PO Box 46096
Escondito, CA 92046-0996

AAA, 128
A&R, 48
A&R representative, 48, 94, 159
"A-B method," 99
accessories (pedal, box, etc.), 73, 88, 110, 114
accommodations, 40, 110, 130, 131, 132
accounting, 117–19, 141, 143
advertising, 162
"A-440," 88
age differences, 3
agents, 2, 17, 19, 21, 24, 25, 26–27, 29, 38–41, 43, 49, 86, 93, 94, 114, 122, 126, 131, 141, 142, 144, 157, 160, 167
album, 51, 67, 161, 162–63
alcohol, 79, 82–83
American Federation of Musicians, 154
amphetemines. *See* uppers
amplifiers, 64, 73, 83, 88, 90, 98, 99, 100, 101, 102, 105, 108, 110, 111, 114, 121, 139
  covers, 101, 110, 114
  fuses, fuse caps, 56, 64, 87, 98
  "heads," 98, 103, 111
Arkansas, 119
arrangements, 9–10, 12–15
audience, 6, 8, 58, 60, 61, 64, 66, 67, 73
auditions, 20
  of new members, 137–38
Austin (TX), 3

ballrooms, 51, 161
"band fatigue," 133–34, 165
band meetings, 4
Bangor (ME), 3
bank, use of, 118, 124, 133
banner, 36–37

barbiturates. *See* downers
bartenders, 23, 55, 56, 63, 83, 113
"basic booking kit," 17–19
bass parts, 13, 93
bass player, 2, 13, 70, 72
beat, 6, 8, 13, 66, 69, 70, 71, 74, 82, 91
Beatles, 12, 75, 164
Berry, Chuck, 8, 9, 65
Big Bopper, The, 9
Biloxi (MS), 3
Bland, Bobby, 8
bluegrass, 162
blues, 74, 162
"Blue Suede Shoes," 9
bookings, 16, 17, 22, 23–24, 38, 39, 141, 143
"Born to Run," 12
Boston (MA), 3
bouncers, 55, 108
breaking up, 122, 165–66
brochures, 34, 35, 36
Brown, James, 7
business cards, 22, 38

calendar, 11, 19, 32, 126, 143
campus tavern, 58
Canada, 126
"Can I Get a Witness," 75
cannon connectors, 114
"cash and carry," 117–18
cash (on the road), 132–33
cash register tape, 26, 44
cashiers check, 59, 133
cassette. *See* tape recorder
CB radio, 129
CD, 14, 161, 163
Cedar Rapids (IA), 3
chalkboard, 140

"Chantilly Lace," 9
Chapel Hill (NC), 3
"Chestnuts," 6, 7
chord changes, 14, 139
club owners, 9, 17, 19, 20, 21, 22, 23, 25, 28,
    29, 38, 39, 40, 41, 43–44, 45, 46, 49,
    52–57, 67, 86, 108, 110, 113, 125, 131,
    140, 153, 154, 157, 161
clubs, 19, 20, 21, 23, 25, 26, 28, 32, 39, 40,
    43–44, 49, 51–57, 59–60, 63, 66, 85, 94,
    100, 103, 108, 113, 123, 125, 131, 140,
    153, 154, 157, 161
cocaine, 79, 80
Cochran, Eddie, 9
Colorado, 3
college work, 24, 25, 39, 51, 57–59, 94
commissions, (agents, managers), 39, 41,
    126, 144
communication, 3, 4, 81, 129, 140
concerts, 36, 49, 51–52, 58, 66, 157, 161
confirming by mail, 20
contacts, 22, 23, 49, 142, 153, 162
contracts, 26, 27–30, 41, 59–60, 110, 131,
    144, 145, 160
copyright, 10
cords, 98, 99 102, 112
Costello, Elvis, 9
counting off, 71
country & western, 8, 162
country rock, 74
cover charge, 44, 45, 54
"covers," 7, 9, 71
credit, 118
credit cards, 118
Creedence Clearwater Revival, 75
crossovers, 8
cue mix, 90
cutoffs, 71, 75

dance music, 6, 60, 74, 75, 86
dances, 58
"Dancing in the Dark," 12
Davis, Miles, 61
debts, 119, 120, 122, 128
demand, 125–26
demos, 35, 94, 158, 161. *See also* tapes
Detroit (MI), 159
Dixon, Willie, 8
DJs, 94
do-it-yourself album, 162–63
"the door," 52, 53
doorkeepers, 55
downers (heroin, etc.), 80, 83
dress, stage, 62, 108
dress codes, 44

drink policy, 54, 110
"Drive My Car," 75
drivers, 127, 128
drugs, 79–83, 109, 133
drum machine, 70
drummer, 2, 15, 70, 71, 88, 111
drum parts, 13
drunks, 52, 112
"dubs," 19, 93, 94

Ellington, Duke, 126
E-mail, 35
engineer, 86, 88, 90, 91, 92, 93, 94, 95
EP, 32, 161
equipment, 56–57, 87, 97–106, 108, 109, 110,
    113–14, 121, 128, 139
equipment truck (or van), 109, 110, 113,
    118, 120, 121, 122, 127, 128, 133, 139
"existential partnership," 118–19

"Fame and Fortune," 75
fans, 43, 44–48, 61, 122
    key, 45, 49
    out-of-town, 45
    subsidies from, 45–46, 122
firing, 135–36, 165
flyers, 24, 26
folk, 51, 61
following, 20, 43–48, 49, 159, 161
food (on the road), 132
fraternities, 24, 58
fronting the band, 63–65
fuse, fuse caps, 56, 64, 87
fuses, power, 98, 111

Gaye, Marvin, 75
gender, 5
gigs, 2, 3, 4, 5, 17, 20, 21, 22, 24, 25, 28, 38,
    40, 49, 58, 106, 108, 110, 111, 125, 129,
    133, 143, 159, 162
goals, 16–17, 21, 25
ground switch, 102, 103
groupies, 46–47
guarantee, 52, 125
guide track, 90
guitar, 72, 88
    acoustic, 91
    electric, 91, 97, 99
    rhythm, 13
guitar player, 3, 71, 73, 87

hashish, 81
"hatred phenomenon," 143–44
hats, 62

headphones, 90, 91
"Heartbreak Hotel," 13
hecklers, 64
heroin. *See* downers
high school dance, 58
hiring, 136–38
home base club, 43–44, 49
"hook," 9, 139
Howlin' Wolf, 8
"Hurts So Good," 75

"I'll Follow the Sun," 12
image, 33–34, 61–62, 65, 79
imitations, 7
incorporation, 119
in-joke, 67
IRS, 123

jams, 67, 82, 95, 139, 157
jazz, 51, 61
"Johnny B. Goode," 8

keyboard player, 2, 121, 165
key change, 6, 74
Key West (FL), 125
King, B. B., 8

language, standard, 3,–4
"Lawdy Miss Claudy," 13
lawyer, 144, 160
leader, 1–2, 62–63, 71, 135, 136
lead parts ("breaks"), 13–14, 75, 88, 89
lead playing, 13–14, 70, 75–77, 88
leads (solos), 13, 69, 70, 75–77, 87, 88
    double, 14, 139
    fills, 14
lead vocalist, 87, 90, 11, 121, 166. *See also*
    singer
"leakage," 90
leasing (truck), 121, 122, 127
letter of agreement, 22, 23
level check, 91
lighting, stage, 62, 111
"lightning rod protection," 143–44
listings, 32–33
"Little Red Rooster," 8
living together, 5, 11
logo, 37
Los Angeles (CA), 48, 144, 159

mailing list, 49
maintenance, of equipment and truck,
    100–02, 103, 113, 127

management contract, sample, 145–52
management deal, 144–45
management services, 38, 39, 159
managers, 2, 21, 119, 120, 121, 141–54, 160, 167
marijuana, 81
master (dubbing), 93, 94, 162
master book, 139
material, choice of, 6, 8, 9, 18, 19, 59–60, 74,
    85–86, 87, 138, 139, 165
    original, 7, 8, 9–10, 16, 17, 63, 86, 158
medleys, 7, 8, 9, 12
Mellancamp, John, 13, 75
"Memphis, Tennessee," 8
metronome, 15, 70, 76, 91, 139
microphones, 88, 91, 99, 100, 101, 102, 103,
    105, 111
    cables, 100, 102, 111, 114
    stands for, 111
"Middle of the Road," 75
mixdown session ("mix"), 89, 92–93
mixers, 58, 103–04, 105, 111, 121
money, handling, 57, 117–24, 128, 132, 143
monitors, 63, 105–06, 121
movement on stage, 64, 65–66
MTV, 157, 161
multitrack recording, 89–90, 91, 92
musicianship, 69–78

name of band, 31–32, 36–37, 58, 63
Nashville (TN), 159
New Hampshire, 41
Newman, Randy, 9
newspapers, 31, 35
New Wave music, 6, 157, 162

office supplies, 38
oldies, 8
Omaha (NE), 125
"Orange Blossom Special," 74
original material. *See* material, original
outdoors, performing, 103
out of town. *See* road, on the
overdubs, 89

pacing, 8, 71, 74, 75
partial payment, 28
partnership, 143
PA system, 63, 66, 67, 70, 99, 100, 101,
    103–06, 111, 119, 121
    columns (cabinets), 57, 103, 121, 122
    component, 104–05
    package, 104
pay, 4, 20, 22, 25, 28, 29, 39, 41, 44, 52, 57,
    58, 113, 114, 138, 143

payment by check, 57, 118
Peoria (IL), 3
Petty, Tom, 13
photos. *See* pictures
phrasing, 76
picks, guitar, 102, 112
picture postcards, 38, 49
pictures, 17, 24, 33–34, 36
pitchpipe, 66
"pocket kit," 101, 112
posters, 31, 36
PR. *See* publicity
Perkins, Carl, 9
Presley, Elvis, 8, 9, 75
press kit, 31, 33–35, 48
press release, 35
Pretenders, 75
printer, 36
producers, 92, 158, 159, 160
production deal, 160
promoters, 158
promotion. *See* publicity
"Proud Mary," 7, 75
psychedelics, 51, 82
    major, 82
    minor, 82
publicity, promotion (PR), 24, 25, 31, 32, 37,
    48, 58, 118, 144, 157, 158, 162
publishers, 160
publishing agreement, 136, 166

radio stations, 8, 9, 31, 32, 94, 158, 161–62
    announcers, 38, 48, 94, 162
rap, 157, 162
rearrangements, 7, 8
record companies, small, 161–62
record deal. *See* recording contract
record promo people, 48, 158
record store personnel, 48
record stores, 157, 162
recording contract, 17, 86, 141, 144, 153,
    157–62. *See also* contracts
recording, multitrack, 86
reference vocal. *See* guide track
rehearsal space, 11
rehearsal studio, 139
rehearsals, 2, 5, 11–13, 14, 155, 87, 89,
    138–40, 158
    "section," 139
    tapes, 15, 70
rentals, truck, 122, 128
repertoire sheet (rep sheet), 19, 33
representation, 142
review, 12
rhythm, 70, 74, 88

rhythm 'n' blues, 8
rhythm parts, 13
rhythm section, 13–14, 139
rhythm tracks, 89
road, on the, 2, 113, 123, 125–34, 140
Road Atlas, 129
"road bands," 126
road management, 141
roadie, 29, 103, 106, 107–15, 121, 131, 143
"Rock 'n' Roll Music," 8
"Rock Me on the Water," 75
"Roll Over Beethoven," 8
Rolling Stone, 48
Rolling Stones, 8, 75, 117

salary, 114, 118, 119
school bus, 127
Seattle (WA), 3
set, 74–75
    building, 8, 74–75
    number of, 22, 23, 51, 53
    planning, 53, 60, 69
set screws, 114
setting up, 56, 87, 110–11
sex, 5
"She Loves You," 12
shocks, 102
short circuit, 102
showcase gig, 17, 159
showmanship, 61, 67
Simon, Paul, 9
singer, 3, 67, 71, 91, 105, 111
sleeping bag, 131
"snake," 111, 121
song, 9, 14, 74
songwriters, 9
sound check, 111
sound system. *See* PA system
spares, 98, 99–100, 112
speaker cabinet, 98, 103, 110, 121
speakers, playback, 92
specialty items, 37
speed. *See* uppers
Spin, 48
Springsteen, Bruce, 12
stage in club, 56, 62, 73, 83, 110
    image on, 66
"standby," 110
stationery, 38
"Stormy Monday Blues," 8
Strauss, Johann, 46
strings, guitar, 72, 87, 88, 100, 102, 102
studio, 12, 85–95, 158, 162
    demo, 86
    home, 19, 95

studio time, 85
suite (motel), 131
"Summertime Blues," 9
"Sweet Little Sixteen," 9

talk (onstage), 62–65, 66, 83
Talking Heads, 75
tape recorder, 12, 15, 19, 87
tapes, 19, 24, 35, 85, 86, 92, 93, 94, 139, 158, 159, 161, 162
 1-inch, 2-inch, 87
taxes, 30, 123–24, 141
  deductions, 123
  diary, 123
tempo ("time"), 15, 70, 82, 139
theft, 56, 57, 120, 143
"The Thrill Is Gone," 8
tool kit, 101–02, 112
"Top 40," 7, 8, 16
tour, national, 17, 125, 157
transportation, 5, 120, 124, 126
traveling emblem, 36–37
truck. *See* equipment truck (or van)
T-shirts, 37, 108, 112
tubes, 98
tuning, 66, 69, 72, 87

tuning device, electronic, 66
tuning fork, 66
"Twist and Shout," 12

union, musicians', 154–55
updates, 8
uppers ("speed"), 79–80

vacation, 133–34, 165
vacation fund, 188
Van Halen, 8
Van Halen, Eddie, 46
vehicle depreciation, 120, 127
Vermont, 26
verses, 9
videotape, 66
vocalist. *See* lead vocalist
vocals, 87, 88, 89
  backups, 14–15, 89
  lead, 15, 89, 90
volume, 67, 69, 73, 83, 103, 104

waitresses, 25, 55, 63, 65, 108, 113
woodshedding, 11, 136
writers, 48, 66, 94